THE REFERENCE SHELF

Volume VII

Volume VIII. $2.40

Volume IX. $1.80

Volume X. $4.20

Volume XI. $6

THE REFERENCE SHELF *(Continued)*

Volume XII. $6

Volume XIII. $6

Volume XIV. $6

Future Issues to be Announced

PLANNED ECONOMY

A Supplement to
INCREASING FEDERAL POWER

Compiled by

HARRISON BOYD SUMMERS
Professor of Public Speaking, Kansas State College

and

ROBERT E. SUMMERS

NEW YORK
THE H. W. WILSON COMPANY
1940

FOREWORD

This volume, intended for use by high school debaters using this year's question, is a supplement to *Increasing Federal Power*, published earlier this year. In that book the general aspects of federal power and its relation to modern life were considered. Since most affirmative debate teams will uphold increased federal power on the basis that it permits more intelligent planning of our national economic system, the compilers of this book have attempted to collect, in this limited volume, the most valuable materials relating to that field from every approach worthy of consideration at this time.

For their kindness in permitting the reproduction of copyright materials which appear in these pages, the compilers are deeply indebted to Messrs. Benjamin J. Anderson, Jr., John B. Andrews, Abraham Epstein, Herbert Hoover, John L. Lewis, Everett Dean Martin, Neville Miller, Dr. Frederic A. Ogg, Burton F. Peek, Arthur Pound, Donald R. Richberg, Thomas L. Smith, L. J. Taber, Robert A. Taft, Eugene P. Thomas, A. F. Whitney, and Daniel Willard; to the editors of *The Annalist*, *The Annals of the American Academy*, *The Bankers Magazine*, *The Commercial and Financial Chronicle*, *The Congressional Digest*, *Factory Management and Maintenance*, *The Magazine of Wall Street*, *Mechanical Engineering*, *New Republic*, *Plan Age*, *Printers' Ink*, *Proceedings of the Academy of Political Science*, *Steel*, and *Vital Speeches*; and to the National Economic and Social Planning Association.

H. B. SUMMERS
R. E. SUMMERS

Wichita, Kansas
November 2, 1940

CONTENTS

INTRODUCING THE PROBLEM

CONGRESS LOOKS AT PLANNING [1]

Among the results of the economic depression . . . has been the development of a widespread discussion among public officials, business men and economists of the possibility of a nation-wide economic planning system whereby economic depressions may, in the future, be avoided.

Brought down to its simplest terms, the general conclusion is that the depression is due to overproduction in both agriculture and manufactures. . . .

The remedy for that, most manufacturers contended, was a curtailment of production. Their argument was that to keep on manufacturing more than they could sell would lead inevitably to bankruptcy. But the reduction of production meant the reduction in the number of employees. This resulted in unemployment. Unemployed wage earners cannot become purchasers and this, it was argued, lowered even further the consuming capacity of the nation and forced further curtailment of production.

Many of the producers argued that the cost of labor was the key to the situation. They pointed out that although we were producing plenty of everything the cost of production was so high that a sales price to bring profit to the producer, was forced to a height consumers refused to pay.

In answer to this statement it was argued by opponents of wage restriction that a wholesale reduction of wages would further restrict the buying power of the public.

Opponents of reduction of production took the position that it was not this last that was required to balance the economic

[1] From "Congress Considers National Economic Planning." *Congressional Digest,* 11:97. April, 1932. Reprinted by permission.

situation, but a more equable distribution of the income from production.

Finally, with a general agreement on all sides that economic conditions were out of joint, there grew the discussion of whether a definite national economic planning system could not be devised which would stabilize industry to the extent that industries could be carried on in a manner which would insure a decent profit to the producer, a decent income to the wage earner, and leave the general public with a decent purchasing power to maintain himself at a decent standard of living.

Dozens of plans have been offered and dozens of books have been written on the subject. The theories range all the way from the Communist theory of Russia and the Fascist theory of Italy, in both of which a central governmental body practically dictates the rules of industry, to the theory of some leading American financiers and manufacturers, that it is impossible to set up any central economic planning system that will operate successfully against the human equation and what they term the inevitable laws of supply and demand. . . .

THE PROBLEM OF PLANNING [2]

The repeated failures of the general processes of business enterprise both in this and other nations during the past century have been the occasion of many proposals for the reconstruction of our political, social, and economic practices and institutions. The devastating results of the present depression, together with the rapid development of Fascist, Communist, and cooperative governments in other countries, have given added emphasis to these proposals. It would require a rather elaborate treatise merely to summarize the many suggestions made to cure our

[2] By Walter Rautenstrauch, professor of industrial engineering, Columbia University. From "Planning for Economic Performance." *Mechanical Engineering.* 58:631-4. Oct. 1936. Reprinted by permission.

present economic ills. In the discussion of many of these points of view one finds repeated reference to the idea of planned economy in substitution for the generally accepted *laissez faire* principle of economic life which Adam Smith popularized in his now classical treatise on *The Wealth of Nations.* It was not until the beginning of the present century that the idea of planning and coordinating operations in manufacturing enterprises was introduced. Since then almost all business enterprises have developed planned procedures, not only in their shops, but also in their offices, merchandising methods, and accounting practices. The terms "shop systems," "budgetary control," and "sales forecasting" were not in general use a quarter of a century ago. Today every business of any consequence uses planning methods to coordinate the work of purchasing, processing, and merchandising. It is quite natural, therefore, that the idea of applying the same technique of planning to our national plant as a whole should come under review. . . .

The subject involves two concepts; planning and economic performance.

The design of a plan to accomplish an economic performance raises this question: What kind of economic performance is desired and in what terms shall it be expressed? Our problem, therefore, begins with the specification of the end results to be attained. It is suggested that a desirable performance of our national economy should accomplish the following results:

1. The most efficient use of nonrenewable material resources such as coal, iron, and gas.

2. The most efficient use, replacement, and additions to renewable national resources, such as the land and its derivatives, wheat, timber, hogs, and cotton. These objectives raise the problems of maintaining and developing physical assets. Much of our so-called prosperity of former days was but the faulty accounting of wasting assets as profits.

3. The growth of the social capital as expressed in the physical, intellectual, and spiritual well-being of every man, woman, and child. This raises the problem of providing those conditions which will assure all persons an opportunity to take part in and contribute to the processes of civilization and culture, and through such participation to derive nourishment for their physical and spiritual developments.

The present processes of civilization have not been operating specifically toward these ends. Our objectives have not been rational because our social philosophy has been faulty. Social conditions are due to social practices and social practices arise from the rules man makes for playing the game of civilization. This game is played by rival teams called private enterprise seeking profit and fortune by hiring for wages the mass of human labor.

Many so-called economic laws which are generally believed to be "natural" laws are no more than the recorded results of man made processes. They are no more natural laws than the baseball rule "three strikes and out" is a natural law. The entire economic framework in which our business processes are set is wholly man made, and there is nothing sacred about it. We have evolved an economic process for operating the nation's business which is based on a false sense of values and the stockholders of the national plant are wondering if they have not been deceived by faulty accounting methods, because of which the real changes in the values of the national assets are not disclosed. It seems, therefore, that the real objective of any economic planning must be such use of our physical and social capital that their values are at least not impaired and preferably increased for the use of future generations. It is hoped and believed by many that the end result of our present procedure is the general well-being of mankind. Others maintain that it has resulted in the exploitation and depletion of our national resources and social capital, and faulty accounting has recorded such liquidation of assets as a net gain.

These differences of opinion warrant a critical examination of our business and social practices to determine what if any basic principles there are upon which a planned procedure for economic development may be founded. . . .

If planned economy is to be successful it must conform in its design and structure to those principles which experience indicates are inherent to successful organized procedure. Accordingly, the plan must be based on:

1. An understanding of the operating characteristics of the functional equipments by which society converts the materials of its environment to its needs, and all of the purposes these equipments serve.

2. An appreciation of the fact that the life-giving principle of an organization lies in the excellence of its equipment for external and internal integration, that is, its nervous system. Society provides itself with its material requirements by its functional equipments for agriculture, forestry, mining, manufacture, and construction. It distributes these through its equipments for transportation, warehousing, and retailing. It facilitates these transactions through its many agencies of money and credit. . . .

If the functional equipments of society are to be maintained in a healthy state so that they can best serve society's needs they must be integrated and their operations coordinated. No sound economic system can be devised on any other principle. No system of government through which planning for economic performance is to be accomplished can be operated successfully in disregard of the foregoing principles of organization structure.

The technical skills with which these many functional equipments have been designed are rightly counted as partial evidence of the growth of civilization. But these industries and institutions serve other than technical functions. They establish the conditions under which people associate with each other, that is, they determine ways of life out of which the culture of the race develops, and they also serve as agencies for distributing the national income, that is, the claims to the goods and services produced. Any plan for better economic performance must also take account of these social and economic functions. We must reorganize the distribution of the national income not only in better and more workable proportions but also as to the ways in which it originates. The functional units of the business process are in a healthy state, individually and collectively, when they operate in harmony with (1) technical, (2) economic, and (3) social principles of interdependent relationships. . . .

The problem now raised divides itself into two main parts— first, setting up a social and economic system which our objective analysis informs us will mean most in social and economic results, and second, devising a practical means of redirecting our present social behavior at minimum social cost. Planned economic performance of any kind is impossible until there are means for carrying out the plan.

Is it too much to expect of mankind that it alter its structure of social organization to make better rules for playing the game of civilization? Are we intelligent enough or are there a sufficient number of enlightened leaders capable of devising proper techniques of social change? My firm conviction is that while the stupidity of man may retard the social organism in its natural tendencies to grow to its destined perfection, it cannot prevent its ultimate accomplishment. Perhaps the present world distress is but the birth pains of a new enlightened age of man.

FASCISM IN PLANNING [3]

If you are going to call everything in the way of collectivist action by economic groups Fascist, we suppose the farm program deserves the designation.

[3] From an editorial in the Des Moines *Register*, May 20, 1938, reprinted in the *Congressional Record*. 83:2179. May 26, 1938.

But let's clear our minds both on the theoretical and practical sides.

After all, the contrast is not between anarchy and fascism, but between workable democracy and fascism. Complete individualism is anarchy. Democracy has never been that. The idea of democracy is the workable maximum of freedom for the individual. That workable maximum varies with conditions. It is one thing in a simple economic and social order—of self-sufficient, subsistence farming, for instance. It is another thing in a complex order, in which each group is dependent on each other great group. . . .

Never have we had a better example than in connection with American agriculture's struggle to put itself on a fair footing with other economic groups.

If the agricultural effort of today, if agriculture's collectivist approach, is dangerously fascistic, so are the things that led to it, the things that made it inevitable.

We mean tariffs. We mean concentrated industry, the quasi-monopoly nurtured by tariffs, and other things. We mean all the rigidities introduced by "capital" into cost structures and price practices. We mean the rigidities imposed by labor— which also flow, we fear, inevitably out of the very nature of the industrial age.

SOCIALISM THE ISSUE [4]

The issue is whether America shall adopt a form of what might be described as state socialism, or, if you prefer the term, state capitalism, or, if you wish to state it in a different way, state centralized government, dominating the economic life of the people. . . . I know of no way to maintain the freedom of the individual under such a system. . . .

[4] By Wendell Willkie, Republican candidate for President, excerpt from a speech at Springfield, Illinois, Oct. 19, 1940. *Christian Science Monitor.* 32:1c. Oct. 19, 1940.

If the United States becomes involved in another war . . . it is my judgment that the national debt will rise to such a point that all the economic instruments of this country will have to be socialized.

OUR CHANGED ECONOMY [5]

The most serious problem confronting the United States has no significant relationship to the European war. It has been with us for some time. To put it baldly, our industrial depressions are tending to become both more frequent and more severe.

In the twenty-year period since 1919 there have been thirteen years in which industrial production at some time fell below 85 per cent of what statisticians calculate as "normal." There were only four such years in the sixty-nine year period from 1850 through 1919. . . .

This demonstrated instability is, of course, merely the outward symptom of trouble somewhere in our economic innards. Economists disagree widely both in their diagnoses of the primary trouble and in their suggested remedies. . . .

It should take only a moment's thought to realize that the higher a material standard of living rises, the greater the inherent tendency toward economic instability. . . .

It seems obvious that any further long term rise in our living standard can come about only through additional expansion of demand for non-essentials. If so, we face a most puzzling dilemma. We desire both a high material standard of living and economic stability, but we apparently cannot have both under the present system of things. Thus far no very convincing solution has been hit upon in the proposals of business organizations; the results of the government's efforts to smooth

[5] By Laurence Stern. From "Our Changed Economy." *Magazine of Wall Street.* 65:278-80+. Dec. 16, 1939. Reprinted by permission.

out the economic peaks and valleys have been quite limited; and there is considerable evidence that the "stabilizing" policies of government, business associations, labor unions and farm groups have in fact succeeded only in retarding economic expansion.

No totalitarian or collectivist approach is acceptable to the American people nor is any idea of relegating government to the role of a village constable and giving full play to so-called natural economic forces either feasible or promising. Therefore, regardless of whether there is a change in political administration at Washington, we shall have to continue a groping search for a better way of life by experiment, compromise and adjustment—hoping that somewhere along this road we shall acquire greater wisdom in our public and private planning.

Meanwhile we might well ponder this question: Are we not putting excessive emphasis on stability and protectionism, inadequate emphasis on the need for maximum expansion of production, employment and purchasing power? Even if we have to take two steps back for each step up, it is better to go boldly forward than to stand still.

ECONOMIC PLANNING DEFINED

THE NATURE OF ECONOMIC PLANNING [1]

There has been a tendency to assume that economic planning always connotes a fully planned economy and a rigid, more or less uniform pattern of political dictatorship. On the other hand, there has been a loose interpretation tending to regard all of the expanding services of government as economic planning. . . .

One economist has written: "Planning involves governmental control of production in some form or other. It was the aim of the liberal plan to create a framework within which private plans might be harmonized. It is the aim of 'modern' planning to supersede private plans by public—or at any rate to relegate them to a very subordinate position." However, the point we are making is that the creation of that framework within which private plans might be harmonized as a part of a liberal program of statecraft, itself involves planning of a high order, even though the precise methods may not be those adopted by non-liberal planners, and itself involves a legislative program for the effective handling of the economic realities of our times that will move us far from the doctrinaire position of laissez faire liberalism. . . . Certainly the kind of a system involved will be a quite different one from that which the original apostles of liberalism started out to defend. But it will be a planned economy, whether well planned or not. . . .

We live now in a planned economy of a rudimentary sort, even though we may not recognize it as such; it represents planning as to the *general* aspects of our economy. By some people,

[1] By Arthur G. Coons. From "The Nature of Economic Planning in Democracy." *Plan Age.* 5:43-9. Feb. 1939. Reprinted by permission.

too, general economy planning is identified only with fascism, national socialism, communism, or the various types of socialism. This association is common but by no means necessary. Many types of economic planning can be distinguished:

1. The development of broad systematic policies—monetary, fiscal, financial, labor—establishing the framework within which production functions in response to private, profit-seeking judgments. . . .

2. A second type would include the first, plus the adoption of a voluntary production planning scheme, advisory only; perhaps with some elements of social pressure such as publicity allowed, but including neither legal nor economic bases for effecting adherence. . . .

3. A third type would include a mixed voluntary-compulsory scheme of production planning wherein producers failing to conform may be penalized by taxes or by withdrawing subsidies—or as in the N.R.A., compelled by law to conform if a segment of the plan is accepted by their trade body. . . .

4. A fourth method is a compulsory plan of production, probably with industry privately owned and possibly under a controlled profit arrangement, with conformity assured by law as well as by the methods of the third type. This is the method of fascism or national socialism. . . .

5. A fifth type must be distinguished from the foregoing, although the first type would be presupposed in conjunction, namely, a mixed public-private economy in which large portions of production, possibly natural resource of basic industries or monopolistic lines of production are socialized in management—perhaps also in ownership—these being coordinated in administration. The private channels of production would be left to adjust themselves to markets as at present. Such a plan conceivably could be developed by a liberalistic government.

6. A public economy in which practically every line of production is socialized in control and management (probably

also in ownership) under central planning. This is state socialism, and may be developed into some more comprehensive program of socialism or communism.

PURPOSE OF PLANNING [2]

The true objective of planning is not stabilization at any
static level, but regularized growth. It is the full utilization of
our powers of production, which are continually growing, in
order that our consumption may grow correspondingly. To
this end the purchasing power of the masses must be maintained and must expand. Viewed from the other side, then,
the objective is the progressive raising of the purchasing power
and the standard of living of the people to the full extent which
our powers of production make possible. Increased production
and a raised standard of living must go hand in hand; neither
end can be gained without the other. . . .

Another major objective is greater equality in the distribution of incomes, increasing the proportion going to wages and
the lowest salaries, to farmers, and to the lower income groups
in general. . . .

We have chosen to advocate planning of the voluntary
sort without giving any public body power to draw up schedules
of production and compel adherence to them. The natural
question with reference to this type of planning is whether it
has power to make any real difference to forces so powerful as
those which topple business against its will from prosperity
into depression.

If we test proposals for planning by asking what they could
do to save the situation if once a major depression got under
way, the answer will be discouraging. But that is not a fair

[2] From the "Progressive Conference Report," during hearings before subcom-
mittee of the Senate Committee on Manufactures, Oct. 22 to Dec. 19, 1931. *Congressional Digest.* 11:104. April, 1932. Reprinted by permission.

test, since the most important work of planning is preventive in character. . . .

Planning can not prevent all disturbances that shake the economic system. What it can hope to do is to mitigate or curb those features of the system which cause disturbances to spread and intensify cumulatively; and to prevent business from getting into such a top-heavy condition that outside disturbances will start it on a long downward slide. Even this will be sufficiently difficult. Private business has not failed, but the *laissez faire* method of keeping people at work and machines at work has failed to accomplish endurable results. It is both logical and urgently necessary to give business the chance to try a different method.

The main hope of results lies in the combination of scientific fact finding directed to uncovering the causes of instability, a standing organization devoted to the problem, and representation of all the interests involved, which between them have a far larger stake in stabilization policies than single business enterprises feel. No one of these above would be sufficient, but from the combination of all of them some results may fairly be expected.

PLANNING BOARDS WITHOUT POWER [3]

The National Resources Committee as it is now constituted has no power whatsoever. It cannot compel any agency, governmental or business or industrial or other, to do anything.

That [compulsion] is not the idea in planning. . . . Planning agencies do not work that way. They are fact finding, coordinating, and advisory—always that and never more than that. They do not desire powers, for they are not administrative agencies. Their function is to plan, to study problems, gather

[3] By H. T. McIntosh of the Albany (Georgia) *Herald,* from a letter to his Congressman, reprinted in Appendix, *Congressional Record.* 84:2124. May 22, 1939.

and correlate information, submit reports to executive heads and legislative bodies, and prepare plans which may be adopted in whole or in part or rejected in their entirety.

The idea of a national or a state planning agency clothed with powers is fantastic. It is repugnant to the whole spirit of planning. . . .

A national planning agency is indispensable to the states. I make that statement without qualification, and out of my knowledge of the situation in at least six states. The present national agency (National Resources Committee) furnishes expert consultant service to state boards, and serves as a clearing house through which all the state boards, as well as regional planning groups, are kept in touch. It is a fountain of planning inspiration. . . .

EXPERIENCE WITH ECONOMIC PLANNING

EXPERIMENTATION UNDER THE NEW DEAL [1]

Many forms of government experimentation have been indulged in by the New Deal. Literally every possible and conceivable form and type of government action for the purpose of interfering with the normal operation of the economic and social order has been attempted during the past five years by the President and his bright young "brain trusters."

A few illustrations of such government experimentation are: Direct control of prices and production; control of production alone; control of prices alone; taxation; government competition with private industry; and the use of government propaganda.

A glaring example of the direct control of production, prices, and wages by the government was the National Recovery Administration. . . . For the first time in the history of our country in an era of peace, the government was attempting to control prices and production for practically all goods and services. . . .

PLANNED CROP CONTROL IN AGRICULTURE [2]

Out of the efforts made during the last decade to improve the position of the American farmer, at least one national policy of major importance seems to be definitely established as a part of our agricultural economy. That is crop control.

[1] From discussion in the House of Representatives by the Hon. Paul W. Shafer of Michigan, in Appendix, *Congressional Record*. 83:2822. June 15, 1938.
[2] From an editorial in the Birmingham (Alabama) *News* of Oct. 13, 1939. Appendix, *Congressional Record*. 85:317. Oct. 16, 1939.

In the light of events in recent years, it is hard to see how we can do without some kind of control over production in the few major crops, particularly cotton, wheat, tobacco, and possibly one or two others. It seems to be the only device whereby ruinous overproduction of these staple commodities can be prevented.

We shall probably continue to have crop control for two reasons. One is that it seems necessary, and the other is that the farmers themselves apparently do not intend to let go of the device, which in general has worked reasonably well for them.

After crop control was first adopted—with the consent of the farmers themselves—prices of the major agricultural commodities rose from the extremely low levels of the worst depression years, and the huge surpluses began to diminish. By preventing too great overproduction and cutting down the surpluses, crop control put agriculture on a sounder and more stable basis. On crops of more moderate size farmers were able to obtain better prices and realize a higher income.

American agriculture was doing better from 1933 to 1936 than it had in years, largely because of crop control. Then in 1936 came the Supreme Court decision which invalidated the Agricultural Adjustment Act, and as a consequence of that the crop control acts were repealed. Immediately, we had overproduction again in the major crops, and prices tumbled. The farmers were almost back where they were before 1933.

In 1937, the first full crop year after the A.A.A. decision and the repeal of the crop-control acts, we grew the largest cotton crop in history, about 19,000,000 bales. In other major agricultural commodities we grew crops that were among the largest on record, if not the very largest.

This was no accident. The crops of 1936 were held to reasonable limits because, even though the A.A.A. was invalidated and the control acts repealed early that year, the machinery for controlling crops then being planted had already been put into operation. Crop control continued in existence for the crop year of 1936.

When almost all effective regulation of crops had been removed, farmers overproduced enormously in 1937, and the resulting collapse of agricultural commodity prices was probably the most important factor in bringing on the business recession which began that year.

Then, in 1938 and again this year, a measure of production control was again established in some of the major crops, though not all, and yields were once more brought within fairly reasonable limits.

The history of the improvements in the agricultural position from 1933 through 1936, the severe setback in 1937 after the invalidation of the A.A.A. and the repeal of the original crop control acts, and the beginning of another upturn in agriculture following the reestablishment of crop control in the last two years, offers convincing evidence of both the need and the effectiveness of regulated production. . . .

After experiences such as the farmers have had in cotton, wheat and tobacco in recent years, it is to be expected that in the future they will generally vote for crop control. As long as the farmers themselves have the decision on production control in their own hands, and as long as a two-thirds majority is required to make it effective, the device will be democratic in nature, and therefore not subject to objection on the ground that it is regimentation by government. . . .

ECONOMIC PLANNING SINCE 1929 [3]

The great disorders in our economic life since 1929 are primarily due to governmental economic planning and, above all, to governmental interferences with the orderly functioning

[3] By Benjamin M. Anderson, Jr., Ph.D., professor of economics, University of California at Los Angeles. From "Governmental Economic Planning." *Vital Speeches.* 6:282-8. Feb. 15, 1940. Reprinted by permission.

of markets, including first, the international markets for commodities and the money and capital markets; second, domestic prices and wage rates. To this should be added the vast increases in taxes and government deficits created by the rapidly growing government functions. I believe that we have in these an adequate explanation of our disorders. . . .

The problem of governmental economic planning is merely part of the general problem of economic coordination and control. . . . The one great instrumentality of economic control and coordination which most clearly and definitely has kept pace with the growth of technology and productive power is the market itself and the system of market prices. And the causes of the greatest evils of the present national and world disorder are to be found in the interferences with the markets by governments under the influence of antiquated doctrines. . . .

I do not believe that, at best, even with government ideally organized for controlling economic life, with an ideal set of officials who are masters of all the knowledge and understanding the economists possess, government could work out a conscious control of the economic life of a great people which would approach in efficiency the unconscious, automatic control which free markets and freely changing prices give. Government, as at present organized in the United States, has difficulty in seeing what the problem of governmental economic planning is. An adequate economic plan must involve the various elements of economic life *in their interrelations*. . . . Effective economic planning would have to be preceded by a complete centralization of our government. Democracy, local self-government, and individual rights protected by the courts would have to be done away with. The reconstitutions of government in Italy and Germany point the way—for those who wish to pursue it. . . .

Government, dangerously strengthened by war, has revived the atavistic economic policies tolerable only in a state of war, and applied them to a world economic life which had grown up under economic freedom in an atmosphere of peace. . . .

When I say that post-war governmental economic planning has had the main responsibility for the economic disorders of the period since 1929, I mean to begin with the developments which preceded the widespread use of the term, "economic planning." . . . The first great post-war action by the American government in interposing barriers to markets, in such a way as to undermine economic equilibrium, was in raising the tariffs in 1921-22. . . The next step was in the employment of our Federal Reserve System in money market manipulation of a new kind and on a vast scale for the deliberate purpose of whipping up prosperity and, above all, for the deliberate purpose of getting out agricultural exports over our tariff walls . . . in 1924 . . . repeated in 1927. It was economic planning. . . .

Part and parcel of this was the placement of foreign loans in the United States, beginning on a really colossal scale in 1924. . . . From the middle of 1924 to the stock market crash in late 1929 the foreign loans offset the high protective tariffs and we, a creditor nation, continued to send out a great excess of exports over imports at good prices. The disequilibrium between agriculture and industry was concealed. Planning offset the evils of prior government interference through that time. But in December of 1929 and in January of 1930 there came an ominous break in the prices of the basic raw materials and of many agricultural commodities, foreshadowing the evils that were to follow.

But governmental economic planning took other forms in the decade of the 1920's. For the first time in our history, the President of the United States and the Secretary of the Treasury assumed the responsibility for the personal conduct of the stock market. . . . Then came more economic planning. In 1929 we created a Farm Board whose function it was to dominate the wheat and other agricultural markets, and it began to work in the autumn of 1929. We got into this game late. Governmentally sponsored pools in Canada, in Hungary, and in Australia had been withholding wheat from the market, leading to a doubling of the visible supply between 1926 and 1929. As our Farm Board bought wheat in late 1929 and early 1930, these other countries sold, taking our export market away from us. . . . Those who condemn the New Deal for its agricultural follies . . . should not credit the New Deal with originality on this point.

Then came another raising of the tariffs in 1930, which intensified to an unbearable degree the difficulties of our foreign debtors in making payments here, and which was followed by a great scramble all over the world to erect trade barriers. . . .

The connection between economic planning and international trade barriers is the connection of a vicious spiral. Each seems to call forth the other; and the more of one you have, the more of the other you call forth. . . . Economic self-sufficiency is a deliberate part of the program of most economic planners. On the other hand, the loss of foreign trade makes a fertile field for propaganda for economic planning. The high protective tariff is the mother of the New Deal. . . .

The essence of governmental economic planning is the belief that government is responsible for the state of business, that it is the duty of government to have full employment at all times, that government must employ special measures with every flagging of industrial activity, that readjustments to correct mistaken economic policies must never be permitted. The call is for more, and more, and more of these activities as the evils growing out of past activities of the kind become more and more glaring.

THE NATIONAL RESOURCES COMMITTEE [4]

For a number of years America has been having alternate floods and droughts; surplus crops and crop shortages; excess materials and not enough houses; wage disputes and stock-

[4] By Duncan Aikman. "Our American Riches." *New York Times,* Jan. 23, 1938. Reprinted in Appendix, *Congressional Record.* 83:313-14. Jan. 1938.

market gyrations; hunger and waste. . . . Finally it became clear that something was basically wrong with the way we were using our national resources. We began to understand that if Americans were to reach the "abundant life" we should have to find some way to coordinate our teeming soil fertility, our enormous technical skills, our manpower and its consuming capacity.

There were two ways of meeting the problems involved. One was to assume, as we did in the past, that time and the breaks of luck would solve them automatically. . . . The other way was to meet the problem head-on, find out what the resources really were, plan to husband those in danger of depletion, speed up development of others and try to fit them all into a plan for healthful use by a reasonably free and democratic economic system. The present government chose the latter method. It set up a National Resources Committee.

Officially the National Resources Committee is just another advisory group of eight members. . . . The committee has no executive power and can neither regulate nor regiment anybody. Its job is to study the resources problems and propose expert solutions before any of those problems reaches the emergency stage. Its proposals may go directly to the President, along with its reports; he may or may not transmit the recommendations to Congress.

As a working organization the committee has a long roll of sub-committees and technical divisions, which include the nation's leading experts recruited from government bureaus, universities, industry, and research foundations. These groups make surveys and do intensive research, and from their findings is arising a new picture of America—a large-scale picture of the land, its people, and its resources in terms of today and tomorrow. . . .

The picture forms the groundwork for the constructive program of the committee. That program is twofold. It involves on the one hand a problem of safeguarding resources against wastage. . . . On the other hand it is a problem of use and enjoyment. . . . It is up to the committee to put its finger on the spot and indicate how improvement can be made.

For this purpose it works through the members and staff experts and technical consultants of its subcommittees in special fields. There are permanent subcommittees on land use and water use, on industry and urbanism, on population and science. Other committees have been called together and are now at work on such specific problems as agriculture, industrial production, the population's consumption requirements, invention and its effect on unemployment. Still other groups will be set up as new problems and fresh emergencies arise. . . . The idea is that so long as the National Resources Committee functions Congress need not try to solve questions regarding the basic economic stability of the nation without benefit of expert testimony. . . .

Meanwhile, in the field of administration the committee has done a straight organizing job, encouraging the establishment of planning boards—local "resources committees"—in every state, in 400 counties and in 1,100 cities and local areas. And it has moved toward the establishment of regional administrative units.

It is no minor task which the Resources Committee has in its keeping, nor one soon to be completed. The scope is enormous. The hope is to gather a store of statistics and fundamental information which may enable us more and more easily to take future crises in our national stride, to absorb revolutionary inventions, to weather economic storms, to adjust our economy to an increasingly elderly population, perhaps even to anticipate and adapt ourselves to radical climatic changes should they come. The attempt is to understand the America of today in terms of the past and present and to view the nation in terms of a future which is measured in decades and generations rather than in months or years or even political administrations.

THE TREND TOWARD FASCISM [5]

The first five-year plan is ended. I am not referring to Russia, Germany, or Italy, but to the good old United States of America.

When the present administration came into power, five years ago, plans were laid for managed economics; and this has been in operation, in this country, more or less, during these past five years.

The essence of the plan was that the government at Washington should assume full responsibility for solving the economic problems of all the citizens. . .

If you stop to think of it seriously, and analytically, you will see that we have had a five-year plan for regulation by the government of practically all human activity in the United States; which, if continued, will put us, more or less, in the same category as the people of Russia, Germany, and Italy. . . .
The present day trend in our country is not so much toward socialism as it is toward fascism; and still a great many supporters of the United States five-year plan seem to believe . . . that all of these regulations are constitutional.

[5] An address by Halloran H. Brown, president of the New York State Horticultural Society. Reprinted in Appendix, *Congressional Record*. 83:231-2. Jan. 17, 1938.

AFTER THE WAR—WHAT?

BUSINESS MUST PLAN [1]

Drastic changes in our economic system must be expected to follow this devastating war. This is a time for serious thinking and planning. Unless we make some effort to anticipate these changes and prepare to cooperate in the rewriting of the theory and practice of our business we may find ourselves operating under unforeseen restrictive influences and unworkable rules. . . .

I believe we must be ready to face new basic and broad changes over which Washington will have no control as a result of this world explosion. Out of necessity new systems of finance and trade will be invented that will strike at the foundation of our business. I don't know what these systems are going to be, but I think we should be looking ahead and using our imagination. We are living in an age when undreamed of events have occurred in incredibly short spaces of time. Almost anything seems possible now.

I am certain that when the changes do come they will be revolutionary enough to upset all our ideas of procedure. We may wake up some day and find that the entire investment picture has changed. A large part of the wealth of the world is tied up in stocks and bonds. These securities have no value unless there is a market for them. It is difficult to see how there can be a market without wealthy classes, which are being wiped out everywhere by "wealth drafting" laws. Other countries have been able to sell confiscated securities in New York. Where could we sell them? There are no other free markets.

[1] By Marshall W. Pask, partner in Mackay & Company, brokers, New York. From a letter to the *Commercial and Financial Chronicle*. 151:187. July 13, 1940.

If there is some sort of new order coming we might as well be realistic about it. If we sit behind a wall of old customs and refuse to see the world changing around us, we will have to take the consequences. Even if we hope for the best we should be ready for the worst.

PLANNED ECONOMY AND FOREIGN TRADE [2]

The export industries have suffered greatly from the appearance of nationalistic economics throughout the world. Centralized control of foreign trade, high tariff barriers, exchange restrictions, quota regulations, export subsidies, import prohibitions and preferential treatments have changed the course of foreign trade. Nationalistic economies aiming to make their countries self-sufficient have changed the nature of the trade of foreign countries. . . . The whims of foreign dictators or extremely nationalistic economies may at a moment's notice completely destroy foreign markets and thereby eliminate the outlets for industries depending on such foreign markets. It is particularly dangerous to expand international trade with methods which involve any sacrifice of American interests since the advantages may disappear through sudden alterations in the policies of foreign countries. It is, therefore, important to reorient American foreign trade policies and to make them more realistic and more deeply aware of the present nature of international trade. We must depend more fully on trade only in materials in which we possess some advantage or which we really need to acquire.

America is interested in the continuance and expansion of foreign trade. Its industries which depend upon such trade can benefit directly by securing new markets. American indus-

[2] By Emil Rieve, president, Textile Workers Union of America. "Economic Nationalism, Trade Barriers and the War." From *Proceedings of the Academy of Political Science.* 19:33-4. May, 1940. Reprinted by permission.

tries which consume foreign products secure their raw materials from other countries. Foreign trade either provides the consumer with goods which he could not obtain in this country or offers them at very attractive prices. Foreign trade cannot be stimulated by any of the current proposals related directly to such foreign demand. . . .

The primary method for expanding this trade must be found in our own national economy; and expanding national income and increased demand for domestic and foreign goods.

LESSONS FROM BRITISH EXPERIENCE [8]

The appointment of Winston Churchill and Labor's entry into the government brought about fundamental changes in Britain. Today all available forces of the nation are united in a concentrated effort to increase the national defense to the attainable maximum. It is true that Britain was compelled to suspend many of her civil liberties for this transitory period. But by doing so, did Britain become a totalitarian state herself in the Nazi sense? The answer to this question is of central importance. Aside from revealing the actual process of developments in Britain, it provides us with information relevant to those crucial problems which the United States also will have to face in due course. . . .

An economic general staff in firm cooperation with the military general staff represents a sweeping transition in the British economic system, as it must necessarily in all countries of liberal economy where private industrialists still determine the volume, quantity and means of production. . . .

Though the objectives of planned economy now encroaching on Britain's economic system are enormous, it must emphatically

[8] By Fritz Sternberg. a contributor to British and American military service journals. From "The Defense of a Free Nation." *New Republic*. 103:15-16. July 1, 1940 Reprinted by permission.

be stated that her total war economy is diametrically opposed to that of the Nazi state. . . . Even though the state's control of national economy increased to a considerable degree, listening to even the most rabid Nazi propaganda broadcasts is permitted and Alfred Duff Cooper, Minister of Information, refused to ban the publication of communiqués by the German High Command in the British press. . . . In other words, Britain has an economy planned for war in which important elements of liberal economy are temporarily suspended, but one that has been decreed and is enforced by the active cooperation of the workers, who voluntarily gave their consent to these emergency measures. . . .

In all essential points the United States faces a different necessity. At present, it is engaged in developing its own war economy from a temporarily narrow military basis. America's present war-economic sector is even less developed than was that of Britain at the time of the Munich conference. On the other hand, the New Deal created certain elements of planned economy which are more distinct than those existing in Britain at the outbreak of the war. In all important products, the United States is considerably richer than Britain. In addition, it possesses enormous labor reserves in the ten million unemployed, as well as plant reserves in its not yet fully utilized productive capacity.

Britain today is compelled to restrict the food and goods consumption of her population, since she is incapable of simultaneously training four million men for the army, executing a gigantic armament program at forced speed and providing the masses with peacetime quantities of consumers' goods. A similar economy would probably not be necessary for the United States, certainly not at this stage of events. . . . There is, however, one pre-condition of a vast further development of planned economy. The broader America's war economy becomes, the more important will be the establishment of an economic general staff, together with a broadening of the state's control of the economy at large.

But let us emphasize once more that the introduction of a considerable war-economy control is by no means identical with making a step toward the creation of a totalitarian state on Hitler's pattern. Of course, such developments may make for totalitarian factors, but only if reactionary forces gain the upper hand during the transition. This, however, can be prevented. Therefore the slogan should not be, "Against planned economy and against war-economic control"; the slogan should be, "For planned economy, for the development of a military economy and a simultaneous expansion of social democracy."

THE PROBLEM OF LATIN AMERICA [4]

The principal danger which the nations of Latin America face today arises out of the dislocating effects of the war and its possible aftermath. Cut off from a large part of their European markets for surplus products, these nations are plagued by economic difficulties which may make them a prey to "fifth column" elements. And should the war end in a German victory, each of these Latin American republics would, by itself alone, be in no position to withstand Nazi economic penetration that might undermine their independence.

The interest of the United States in the independence and stability of the twenty other republics of this hemisphere does not rest on a sentimental basis. The establishment anywhere in this hemisphere of a government ready to take orders from the totalitarian dictators would be a menace to our own safety. It is, therefore, scarcely less important for us to safeguard those nations against economic bludgeoning by a triumphant Reich than to build a navy capable of warding off any invasion of this hemisphere.

[4] From an editorial in the *Washington Post*. Reprinted in Appendix, *Congressional Record*. 86:16105. Aug. 19, 1940.

PLANNING NOT ENOUGH [5]

Before the war the American government attempted to maintain its trade in Latin America by the trade agreements, which in principle and method are the antithesis of German commercial policy. . . .

Limited results from the trade agreements program . . . encouraged the adoption of other measures. The Export-Import Bank used government credit to finance our exports and to support the exchange position of certain of the countries. The Reconstruction Finance Corporation offered financial cooperation to develop enterprises in Latin America. A resolution of the Panama Conference in September 1939 created an Inter-American Financial and Economic Advisory Committee consisting of twenty-one experts, one from each of the American republics. . . . The Inter American Financial and Economic Advisory Committee also drafted a project for an inter-American bank. . . . To these measures is now added the proposal of an inter-American joint marketing organization. . . .

Since the United States is unable to absorb Latin American surplus products in the ordinary course of trade, other means are sought to offset the power of the regional economy of Nazi Germany; the other means visualize a competing regional economy embracing North, Central, and South America. The argument runs that an inter-American cartel, by buying and marketing the surplus commodities of the Latin American countries, would permit the Americas to organize effectively their bargaining power. . . .

Difficulties in the way of the success of the cartel are many, and they are not minimized by those who are responsible for the proposal. It would be a long step toward the acceptance

[5] By William S. Culbertson, former member of U.S. Tariff Commission, now head of the department of economics, Georgetown University. From "Economic Defense of the Americas." *Annals of the American Academy.* 211:188-96. Sept. 1940. Reprinted by permission.

of the very authoritarian methods which we deplore in Europe. . . .

A marketing cartel in fact presupposes a common desire of the American countries for economic defense; it presupposes a political understanding sufficiently definite to convert that desire into action. If one or more of the countries say that they do not want to be defended from Nazi economic methods, then what—? . . . What will we do if one or more American countries join with a non-American country to nullify the Monroe Doctrine? For more than a century we have comforted ourselves by thinking that this could not happen. But what if it did? . . .

The proposal of the inter-American marketing organization has in its favor that it has dramatized the crisis which we *may* . . . have to meet. But on second thought—on the morning after, as it were—we have the disillusioning emotion that the solution is too simple; that limited application of the idea here or there . . . may be useful, but that only as a desperate measure of self-defense should we embark on a scheme to create a gigantic monopoly of the export trade of the Americas. . . .

It is only as a temporary measure that anything can be said in support of the marketing cartel. . . . But it might be one of the answers, and distasteful as it might be we might have to accept it as the least of several evils.

But the tragedy of a proposal such as the inter-American marketing organization is that it plays into the hands of those reformers who oppose the system of private enterprise and who favor government control and operation. In this country they are the advocates of the very methods which the marketing cartel would be set up to oppose. They argue plausibly, but in a spirit of surrender, that government-controlled foreign trade can be met only in kind. They blame private enterprise in foreign trade and finance as they have blamed it in domestic business, and their objective is to extend the New Deal technique to foreign economic relations. . . .

Under the administration of President Roosevelt the principles and methods of the trade treaties of Mr. Hull have been almost the only vigorous expression of the system of private enterprise. They still should remain the norm from which departures like the marketing cartel, if adopted in any form, should be considered only as a temporary concession to collectivism. . . .

Social planners find in a world at war a happy hunting ground. We should therefore be vigilant to distinguish between temporary governmental projects, perhaps rendered necessary by depression or war, and the system of free enterprise which releases man's productive powers and gives scope to his creative genius. . . .

What I'm trying to say is that the postwar world cannot be rebuilt by marketing cartels, state loans, subventions, and relief. By these and other governmental means we could patch up a sort of existence, but an impoverished world will ask for something more. It will ask for an economic system which will release the creative powers of man and which will provide economic stability and a degree of prosperity necessary for peace and for free democratic institutions.

PLANNING LEADS TO DICTATORSHIP [6]

In every case before the rise of dictatorships there had been a period dominated by economic planners. Each of these nations had an era under starry-eyed men who believed that they could plan and force the economic life of the people. . . . They exalted the state as the solvent of all economic problems.

These men thought they were liberals. But they also thought they could have economic dictatorship by bureaucracy and at

[6] By Herbert Hoover, address before Republican National Convention, Philadelphia, Pa., June 25, 1940. Reprinted speech, p. 7-9.

the same time preserve free speech, orderly justice and free government. . . .

These men were not Communists or Fascists. But they mixed these ideas into free systems. It is true that Communists and Fascists were round about. They formed popular fronts and gave the applause.

These so-called liberals shifted the relation of government to free enterprise from that of umpire to controller. Directly or indirectly they politically controlled credit, prices and production of industry, farm and labor. They devalued, pump-primed, and inflated. They controlled private business by government competition, by regulation and by taxes. They met every failure with demands for more and more power of control. . . .

When it was too late they discovered that every time they stretched the arm of government into private enterprise, except to correct abuse, then somehow somewhere men's minds and judgments became confused. At once men became hesitant and fearful. Initiative slackened, production in industry slowed down.

Then came chronic unemployment and frantic government spending in effort to support the unemployed. Government debts mounted. And finally government credit was undermined. Out of the miseries of their people there grew pressure groups— business, labor, farmers, demanding relief or special privilege. Class hate poisoned cooperation. . . .

It was all these confusions which rang down the curtain upon liberty. Frustrated and despairing, these hundreds of millions of people voluntarily voted the powers of government to the man on horseback as the only way out. They did it in the hope of preserving themselves from want and poverty. . . .

FAVORING ECONOMIC PLANNING

THE CHANGING RESPONSIBILITY OF DEMOCRACY [1]

We live today in a world which is still seeking a way of responsible action, and the difficulties involved have multiplied increasingly in the last quarter century. The turn of the wheel has brought us to a series of experiments in group or collective responsibility throughout the world. . . . In this day of governmental action and state intervention, it may be worth our while to pause the while to examine and re-examine the challenge of this problem of responsibility in its several aspects. . . .

It seems obvious that government eventually will be responsible for such undertakings as those who control it declare to be in the general interest and for the general welfare. There is little possibility of doing what so many have tried to do—classify and pigeonhole so-called governmental functions, setting them down as more or less hard and fast judgments eternally applicable. . . . Doubtless we can all agree that there are some functions necessary to government, functions which if not performed leave us without government. There are some also which cannot be performed by government. . . . Particular governments at particular times and under particular circumstances discover particular things which must not be left undone if there is to be a government and an orderly society. Again these same governments find that certain things cannot be done if revolution is to be avoided. . . .

The whole problem becomes even more complex when under a popular government we venture into the field of control.

[1] From an address by Clarence A. Dykstra, president of the University of Wisconsin and director of the draft, Dec. 28, 1938. *Congressional Record*. 84: 151-7. Jan. 16, 1939.

Insofar as government is a device for doing certain things, it cannot be responsible to itself alone. . . .

We have just experienced an era of government action new for its swiftness and comprehensiveness in American history. We developed new government authorities with an almost complete disregard of all principles of design or of responsibility. Because of this experience and its disappointments in so many directions many have come to see that our governmental establishment does require some accommodation. . . .

We are faced with a very real dilemma. We can equip our government to meet the manifold tasks which we force upon it, and thus develop responsibility, or take the position that no matter how urgent or necessary public action may seem to be, we dare not allow the government to undertake the responsibility. . . .

The dictators have taught us at least two things: That there are no guarantees worth while in the modern alternative to democracy and that people are willing to make great sacrifices—yes; even to their immediate freedom—for announced desirable economic and social goals though their attainment may take many years. . . .

There can be no question that democracy today is being asked to take a responsibility for which originally it was unadapted. The concrete institutional goals for which our early democracy crusaded had to do with personal freedoms and guarantees against governmental interference. It assumed that responsibility for the general welfare could run to the people themselves without much common political action through governmental mechanisms. Today the general welfare and even those individual rights to life and the pursuit of happiness depend in a much greater degree on cooperative efforts through the only agency which is common to all the people, their political establishment.

To perpetuate democracy and responsible government we are faced with certain imperatives:

1. We must discover and proclaim a social and economic program which will provide for Americans the essence of

economic security and the personal freedoms which were inherent in our earlier system of democratic opportunity. . . .

2. We must accept the principle that the common agent of the popular will—the people's government—will be forced to undertake as public functions what the common need requires. The state of the arts, the distribution of natural resources, the organization of our economic life, work opportunities, and the accepted standards of living all will play a part in the determination of what this common need is.

3. We must make a conscious and continuous attempt to adapt the structure of our government to the changing environment in which political institutions work. . . .

4. We must recognize that, in spite of theoretical divisions of the field of governmental power, many of the problems facing our people have become national in their scope and they must be met in some large part by a national attack. No amount of rationalizing or reasoning from precedent will change this fact.

5. We must promote an understanding of the democratic method and its implications. . . .

To those then who maintain the faith, to those who still believe in representative government I suggest that the American people are at this moment in dire need of a social goal to which they can aspire with confidence, a governmental structure which can meet the strains and stresses now and in the future to be put upon public agencies and a citizenship which can be trusted to act with responsibility in the premises.

THE DEAD PAST [2]

There are those who still tell us we ought not to plan our future, that we ought to take refuge in the good old practices and precepts of the past when all seemed well. That is a

[2] An address by Hon. Henry Morgenthau, Jr., Secretary of the Treasury, June 16, 1938. Reprinted in Appendix, *Congressional Record*, 83:3036. June 15, 1938.

perfectly comprehensible attitude. But it is the dream thinking of beaten men who seek solace in the surroundings and associations of a less troubled time in the hope of recapturing the past. The past will not return. We cannot turn the clock back. We live in different times, and history confronts us with new problems that the past had no need to solve and cannot solve for us.

THE NECESSITY FOR PLANNING [3]

Economic planning came into prominence eight years ago when there was a widespread feeling of urgency and impending disaster. . . . One sector of an economy cannot grow in scale without affecting related sectors. Banking and financial organization have grown to accommodate—and control—industry. Labor, unable to bargain individually with corporations, has organized to bargain collectively. Farmers, unable to consolidate through corporate devices or trade associations, have sought organization from the hands of government. . . . Even the consumer, sensing his incapacity to deal individually with organizations, seeks formal representation through government, or forms cooperatives and shopping leagues. In short, the individual is ceasing to act independently and directly as an economic agent, but, in association with those who share common interests, acts indirectly through collective enterprises, and accepts the regulatory controls of their procedures. An atomistic society is being transformed into a society of organizations. . . .

Regardless of class or interest, the majority seems to seek forms of organized control. Because of these influences, interventionism and restriction have become dominant economic policies in large-scale administered industries.

[3] By E. J. Coyle, Member Board of Trustees, N. E. S. P. A. From "Democracies Also Must Plan." Planning Pamphlets, No. 1. p. 3-20. National Economic and Social Planning Association. May, 1939. Reprinted by permission.

With the growth of our industrial economy, there has developed managerial jurisdiction over prices. A free market price system is being displaced by an administered and predetermined price system. . . . Although many consider that these signs point in an ominous direction, the fact is that administrative control of production and price is with us—and frequently by the consent and will of government. As the great depression became more severe, the problem of unemployment became the supreme problem of most of the governments of the world. . . .

When fiscal policies, and even management of currencies, proved ineffective as business restoratives, it became necessary to turn to more direct measures for influencing and determining production and prices. State expenditure has developed step by step from an expedient designed to stimulate private investment into an end in itself. State responsibility for national defense has been extended to the internal defense of the national welfare. Once accepting the responsibility of mitigating the insecurity of the individual, it seems that the state must strive to minimize business fluctuations and to maintain national income.

It is no accident that many measures of the New Deal have affected the financial world. The fundamental power for managing an economy rests on the control of the capital markets. . . . Although government measures of recent years represent in a large part nothing more than the logical extension of well-established principles, there is growing recognition that these extensions necessitate the positive task of integrating the economy. Given the activities undertaken, demand naturally arises for government consciously to formulate more comprehensive economic policies. To achieve greater balance among the various parts of the economy and to integrate the national activities as a whole becomes the principal function of government. Any concept of a mechanical self-regulating society that excludes the state as an agency of conscious direction and change is obsolete. . . .

Any reading of the world press makes it obvious that the increase in government intervention to protect the national economic systems has led to the growth of nationalism. It seems inevitable that it should do so, at least at first. But the paradox of the present situation is that the greater the nationalism and isolation, the more imperative it becomes for nation to imitate nation. Totalitarian aggression forces an organized defense, both economically and politically. In the remaining democracies one sees that the organization of national capacities to produce has become the most urgent necessity of public policies. It is the recognition of this reality which, for example, causes the long time liberal London *Economist* to state: "The one fatal mistake would be to put off the task of efficient organization because it is associated, perhaps wrongly, in the public mind with compulsion. Organization we must have—voluntary if possible, compulsory if not." Because totalitarian countries are now able to control their national life according to their concepts of national needs, other countries are obliged to initiate controls.

The United States cannot isolate itself from the impact of organized force. What is happening elsewhere in the world compels this government to seek a better managed economy at home. . . . These impacts from abroad should not be considered, however, as changing fundamentally the direction in which our economy is moving; they are merely pressures accelerating the process of organization.

The evidence of direct observation reveals that the United States is developing an administered, managed economy in which a large proportion of our economic life is governed according to the administrative decisions and controls of private and public authorities. An inventory of the structure of our American economy reveals that the real world is becoming increasingly a managed world. . . . The problem of organization on which all questions focus is that of democracy. A real challenge exists in whether or not democratic processes can be extended and adapted to the emerging administered structure of society. . . .

It seems that government must be given the responsibility of participating in the administration of organized industries. The direction of policies regarding production and prices is a matter for public representation and action, and the appropriate mechanisms to give that representation need to be devised. Few, if any, industries are now organized so as to be capable of undertaking any responsibility for the way their operations affect the national economy.

It does not follow that all economic enterprise must fit into an administered pattern. Because the trend has been towards an administered economy does not imply that it should engulf the entire economy. . . .

Much discussion of recent years has revolved about the question of planning. "We have talked as if the real issue was *to plan or not to plan*, and the people have taken sides for or against planning." The fact is that whether we shall plan or not is no longer the issue. That question has been decided by the flow of events. Planning is necessary if we are to organize ourselves for action. . . . The real issue is in what manner we shall plan, for what purposes, and to whose benefit. . . .

Organization is indispensable for growth, and we seem to have reached a point beyond which further growth is impossible without further organization. . . . To achieve this more effective organization will require the inter-linking of governmental and industrial planning.

Planning in industry has stopped at the borders of individual companies, and planning in government has hardly penetrated the industrial boundaries. Our economy is criss-crossed with "no-man's lands." The organization problems of today and tomorrow arise from these gaps which separate company from company, industry from industry, and industry from government. Efforts at a cooperative administration must be focused on the intra-industry area, as between concerns within each industry, and the inter-industry area, as between major industries and between government and industry. These areas must be bridged if we are to obtain community of effort. Not until the objectives and mechanics of coordination are evolved will our economy be able to function at its maximum capacity. . . .

As a technique, planning is independent of any particular form of social organization or political theory. As a process and procedure, "it is neither good nor bad in itself; but good or bad according to the ends sought, motives that rule, methods and results obtained." A democracy and an autocracy can both utilize a planning technique. . . . Democracies must learn to plan, and the planning process must be democratically applied to social ends which advance the welfare of the individual. The end of all planning is not the perfection of a process, but the creation of greater opportunities for human development.

UNBALANCED AMERICAN ECONOMY [4]

In those limited areas wherein democratic theories and processes still survive there is an effort to defend them by two major methods: first, by organizing the economic power and the man power of each nation into a military force able and ready to protect it against aggression and eventual domination by another nation of menacing military power; and, second, by controlling the domestic economy so as to make effective use of all the man power, machine power and natural resources available in order to provide the highest possible standard of living for the greatest number of people and thus avoid resort to the totalitarian scheme. . . .

Our economic system is working badly because of a defect which is easy to state but difficult to correct. We have not established the ways and means of cooperation between business managers, workers, property owners, and the government which are necessary to maintain continuous reliable production and

[4] By Donald R. Richberg, former chairman, N.R.A. From "Security Without a Dictator." *New York Times.* Jan. 1940. Reprinted by permission.

exchange. Whether we can do so is the most fundamental issue in America today.

Our trouble is that we cling to a traditional faith developed in a pioneering civilization that ended about fifty years ago— a faith in the independence and self-sufficiency of any hard-working American citizen. We cling to the faith that under a self-balancing system of private property ownership and free competition every man will be able to earn about the living to which his abilities entitle him. The truth is that the industrial system is no longer self-balancing, which is amply proved when millions of men are jobless, suffering for want of the products for which they would exchange their own products if they were put to work. A self-balancing economy has been destroyed, not by lawmaking but by industrial progress.

For at least fifty years most of us have been living in an interdependent world in which no man can stand alone, in which all men, rich and poor, are dependent every day upon the services of thousands of other men for the necessities of life, a world in which a large majority of our people earn their living by using property which they do not own and by working for other people. That is the present situation not only of industrial workers but also of business men, big and little, and of the majority of the agricultural workers.

THE REAL THREAT TO DEMOCRACY [5]

The dictatorships do not seriously threaten us by direct attack; nevertheless they are a menace to American democracy in two important ways. In the first place, they may in their program of imperial expansion precipitate a general European war. Such a conflict is almost certain to become a world war,

[5] By Edmund E. Day, president, Cornell University. From "What Really Threatens American Democracy?" *Vital Speeches.* 5:372. April 1, 1939. Reprinted by permission.

with our own country sooner or later a participant on the side
of the democracies. In the prosecution of such a war we should
almost certainly have to abandon for the time being all pretense
of maintaining democratic ways of living and transacting business. For the duration of the war, the United States would
go authoritarian, like the opposing dictatorships. What would
happen afterwards to the form of American government remains
to be seen. Would democratic ways of life be restored?
Nobody knows. Therein lies one of the dilemmas of democracy
. . . to fight or not to fight, with the probable loss of democracy
either way. . . .

There is still reason to believe, however, that the major
economic problems of the day can be solved under democratic
procedures; that a larger measure of wise forward-planning and
of subsequent effective control is requisite is self-evident.

NECESSITY FOR COLLECTIVE DEMOCRACY [6]

Even if Hitler can be stopped, the day of the nation-state is
over. The small nations that remain after the war will become
satellites of some large and powerful empire. We are entering
on a new imperialism, in which whatever may be true of the
outworn doctrine of sovereignty, the surviving economies will
not be national economies, but continental or hemispheric. Germany and its satellites will constitute one; Russia and its satellites
another; Japan will be the center of a far eastern constellation;
America, Latin America, and Canada—the center of a far western.
Within each economic unit there has been, and will continue
to be, a movement toward running the economy as a planned
whole through state intervention in all the major decisions.
Planning has become the new operative. . . .

[6] By Max Lerner, professor of political science, Williams College, from an
address at Cambridge, Mass., July 30, 1940. Reprinted in Appendix, *Congressional
Record.* 86:15860.

I hope we have learned that unless an economic system can give effective security to the masses of people, they will become the stamping ground for political adventurers, using ideas as destructive weapons. I hope we have learned that whether in peace or war only the well-organized and well administered society can survive. I hope that we have learned that the achieving of economic security involves a heroic effort of the collective will, and what will seem to many almost a revolution in the economic structure. . . .

We have a war economy and will have it, willy-nilly. We are bound to have a vast increase in the size of our administrative machine. The problem is whether we shall try to do all this while maintaining "business as usual" and our ideas as usual—or whether we will take the affirmative and revolutionary energies of men and turn them into the channels of a new collective democracy.

SOCIAL ENGINEERING OR CONFLICT?[7]

The cost of not thinking ahead is now too high for any nation to afford. Neither peace nor prosperity comes to those who persist in thinking "too little and too late." We have repeatedly seen in recent years how confusion of policies and stumbling opportunism can dissipate the inherent strength of democracies.

We cannot rest on a wish that everything will turn out all right. Uncertainty, long continued, becomes intolerable, and men forsake democratic processes by resorting to force. There must be—and there is—a better way. Democracies must learn to plan.

Planning is not a theoretical technique; it is a tested skill, and a part of the procedure of many industries and public

[7] From "Plan," a pamphlet issued by the National Economic and Social Planning Association, Washington, D. C.

agencies. Scientific planning implies the choice and definition of objectives; research into the pertinent facts; the selection and coordination of available means; and the securing of co-operation and understanding from all concerned. Policies thus clearly defined and clearly understood can be vigorously pursued.

Our present need is to assemble the knowledge we have and to organize it for useful ends. To bring together all the threads that enter into modern economic problems requires a combination of the broadest learning and the deepest insight. No one man and no one field of knowledge can possibly supply all the answers. There must be group action, group thinking and group contribution toward the common welfare.

Out of united effort will arise a program. Not a Utopia, not a panacea, not a blueprint imposed from above—but the means, shaped and determined by knowledge, to achieve an objective. Planning as a social engineering process for the solution of problems should appeal to the realism of reasonable men interested in growth rather than in conflict.

ECONOMIC PLANNING VERSUS DICTATORSHIP [8]

It is true that the Soviet Union, Germany, Italy, and Japan have a high degree of economic planning, associated with a low degree of what we call free institutions. Is it because of their economic planning that free institutions are lacking? In most of these countries free institutions never were solidly established; so it is impossible to contend in those cases that economic planning destroyed free institutions. Furthermore, the collapse of such free institutions as they had was associated with world wide economic instabilities, with the results of war, and with war preparation. Their present comparatively large

[8] By Eugene Staley, associate professor of International Economic Relations, Fletcher School of Law and Diplomacy. From "What Types of Economic Planning Are Compatible With Free Institutions?" *Plan Age.* 6:36-9. Feb. 1940. Reprinted by permission.

amounts of economic planning in most cases *followed*, or at least did not precede, the development of dictatorship. Instead of concluding that economic planning tends to cause dictatorship it seems more reasonable to conclude that both political dictatorship and certain types of economic planning may arise out of the same set of causes.

The whole argument based on an apparent association between planning and totalitarian dictatorship is essentially one of "concomitant variations" or correlation. In logical form it runs: "Where you find a greater degree of economic planning, as opposed to market coordination, there you are less likely to find free institutions." But how would the Scandinavian countries fit into such a picture? The study of Sweden should be commended to those who find themselves growing dogmatic about the incompatibility of all types of economic planning with free institutions. Sweden's institutions are certainly free and appear to have been getting progressively more so at the same time that economic planning has been on the increase in such forms as monetary management, socialist housing schemes, strong trade unions, state competition with business as a means of controlling private monopoly, a strong cooperative movement also challenging private monopoly, and planned programs of public works to counteract depression. Australia and New Zealand might also be cited as instances where exceptionally large amounts of planning co-exist with free institutions. . . .

It is argued that measures of economic planning feed on themselves and lead on inevitably to more and more such measures, until the end result is totalitarian planning. In other words, there can be no stopping, once you substitute some conscious control for some of the functions of the market. This argument, applied indiscriminately to all types of planning, as it has been by some writers, seems untenable in the light of plain facts. Some types of planning may forestall the necessity of other measures of intervention —for example, intelligent monetary management. The public school system in this country is a large economic undertaking run by state ownership, and it has managed to mesh quite well with private enterprise systems; far from destroying free enterprise, it helps free enterprise to work more efficiently. . . .

Not all kinds of economic planning imperil free institutions, nor will we be saved by just any kind. Our troubles may come, not from too much conscious economic management or too little, but from too much in the wrong places and for wrong purposes and at the same time not enough in the right places and for right purposes. This paper has suggested five principles as a guide in shaping measures of conscious economic coordination that will keep the environment as favorable as possible for free institutions. First, all planning measures should be specifically designed for operation in a "mixed system," a system in which a planned sector and a competitive market sector exist side by side and mesh together. Second, economic planning should be positive and adaptive, not restrictive and rigidifying. Third, economic planning must take into account the interests of all who are affected; it must not be conducted merely for particular interest groups, such as groups of producers. Fourth, economic planning these days must not be exclusively national or nationalistic; otherwise it will lead to bigger economic conflicts and to wars. Fifth, economic planning will be compatible with free institutions only in an environment of stable peace, which means that we must take in hand the problem of building some system of world government if our economic planning in the future is to be for the welfare of people instead of for fighting power and war.

TOWARD WORKABLE PLANNING [9]

Planning is in a certain sense as old as man himself, for the sustained effort of trying to control natural and social forces in definite ways and along definite lines is essentially human.

[9] By René de Visme Williamson. From "A Theory of Planning." *Plan Age.* 5:33-42. Feb. 1939. Reprinted by permission.

. . . During the early years of the Roosevelt Administration, the concept of planning reached the peak of its popularity—in the United States at least—and became a by-word on everybody's lips. The suddenness of its general debut and the strength of its appeal during a period of depression stripped it of its exclusive character and, as a result, it became vague and formless. It seemed that another "ism" with a new ending had made its appearance. Then, a wave of conservative feeling branded planning as "socialism" and "regimentation" with such success that its name was dropped as quickly as it had been adopted. . . .

It is obvious that the very expression "to plan" suggests a conscious and deliberate purpose. To act intelligently and rationally, an individual must have a clear objective in mind. . . .

There is no doubt that any sort of planning absolutely requires the services of competent scientists and technicians. The relevant facts must be known, difficulties foreseen, consequences carefully weighed, and the accumulated knowledge systematically assembled into a workable program. This particular element of the concept of planning is the best known of all and therefore needs least elaboration. In fact, *planning* as such is a mixture of scientific research and program making. The work of the many planning boards which have sprung up all over the United States is proof of the fact that the technical aspect of planning is well understood. Nevertheless, the failure of most planners to perceive the important place of ends in a planned economy has not been without regrettable consequences. Actual attempts at planning—like that undertaken in the petroleum industry under the N.R.A. code—have shown that the indiscriminate collection of any and all facts does not constitute planning. It is not possible to turn a body of investigators loose and tell them to comb the country to see what they can find and then expect that the state will be in a position to act intelligently. The outstanding example of this sort of procedure—or lack of it—was President Hoover's Committee on Social Trends. The

Committee unearthed much interesting material, but no action could be taken by the government on the basis of that report. Not only the formulation of an adequate program, but also the collection of facts that give it substance, are in considerable measure dictated by the thing one is trying to do. The Petroleum Administrative Board, for example, frequently discovered *what it needed to know* only *after* it proposed to undertake some action. Important as it is, research is essentially secondary. . . . It follows that planning is a creative and not a merely mechanical process. . . .

Whatever area of economic life is planned must be under one final authority lest a hopeless and aggravating tangle of activities be the result, and there must be *singleness of end.*

PLAN, BUT WITHOUT CONTROL [10]

I am clear in my own mind that this country is not ready for the type of centralized control which would come from any central economic planning body with power. I think that not only is it not ready for it, but I sincerely hope that it never will be ready for it, because I should consider it the next step to sovietism in its implications. Some measure of control will always be necessary. . . . Some measure of control and perhaps an increasing measure of control may be necessary in the future, just as our police forces get more complicated with the increasing complexity of cities. I mean control in the sense of giving orders; quasi judicial bodies controlling decisions. I regret every extension of the tendency to centralize control of the decisions —it may be a proper price to pay for the thing to be accomplished, and then I am in favor of it—but I regret the extension of centralized control because I do not think that is the way to run 125,000,000 people, and I do not think it is the best

[10] By Wallace B. Donham, dean, Graduate School of Business Administration, Harvard University. From hearings before Senate Committee on Manufactures, Oct. 22-Dec. 19, 1931. *Congressional Digest.* 11:115. April, 1932. Reprinted by permission.

way to get the best and most progressive results out of the complicated situation arising in a very complicated civilization. I think we must stimulate individual initiative, and I am wholly opposed to the principle of control in any economic planning situation, and yet I believe that economic planning is of the essence to the continuance of our civilization.

INDUSTRY CAN'T PLAN ALONE [11]

Planning for the future is the only efficient way of running industry. A system of planned industry would save us from wasting billions of our national income. A plan providing employment for all persons willing to work, maintaining the standard of living and laying aside reserves will not benefit any one group alone. It will give security and comfort to the country as a whole. . . . Any program of that kind would have to be national in scope, and to have it national in scope there is no existing agency. . . .

It is impossible for industries to do it alone. They won't do it; they have not done it, and they will not do it. The only power that can put it into effect is governmental action. There have been promises as to what industry will do. We know that nothing constructive from the larger point of view was done when they were in position to do it. . . .

NEED FOR LABOR-PLANNED ECONOMY [12]

It is clear that democracy cannot continue to exist unless it can adjust its economic operations so that it shall not cast out, as it has today, 13,000,000 workers from its productive system.

[11] By Sidney Hillman, labor leader, and member of various national labor advisory boards. From hearings before Senate Committee on Manufactures. Oct. 22-Dec. 19, 1931. *Congressional Digest*. 11:112, 114. April, 1932. Reprinted by permission.

[12] From the report of John L. Lewis, chairman of the C. I. O., to the first constitutional convention of the C. I. O., Pittsburgh, Nov. 14, 1938. p. 26, 35. Reprinted by permission.

With that amount of unemployment the economy is only half alive. Such an economy cannot long continue.

We well know that the nation can provide employment for all its citizens. We know that in doing so it can guarantee a national income which would provide an average of anywhere from three to five thousand dollars a year to every productive worker. The difficulties that stand in the way of the realization of such a welcome state are false and artificial. The workers are available, the plants and productive equipment stand ready, and no one doubts that there is a desire to use these products. . . .

It is becoming obvious that full production in a stable economy can be created only by intelligent direction which has the power and the will to coordinate all economic controls towards that single end. Such central direction must necessarily come from government. Intelligent direction also of necessity means planning toward the future. One of the serious defects of the economic measures of the present administration has been the failure to coordinate and plan its economic program over an adequate period.

The goal of full production and full employment is one to which it would be difficult to find open opposition. It is clear, however, that there are many who oppose that goal through seeking special interests. Only labor, representing the majority of the people, can guarantee a continuous movement towards full production. Labor must have a strong voice in the government and in the agencies of the government which administer a sound economic program to guarantee that such a program shall not stagnate or be perverted.

FUNCTIONS OF PLANNING BOARDS [18]

We need to give more thought to the subject of planning. When our Oregon State Planning Board attempted to get a

[18] From an address by E. B. McNaughton, president of the First National Bank of Portland, Oregon, at a meeting of the Seattle Chamber of Commerce, April 28, 1939. Appendix, *Congressional Record*. 84:2156-7. May 23, 1939.

renewal of its appropriation from the last session of the legis-
lature it failed. This failure manifestly was due to a misunder-
standing of what planning means. Planning is not something
that is connected with the Democratic Party, or with impractical
idealists. It is as fundamental and as necessary today as a correct
balance sheet and forecast in your own business. . . .

The planning board primarily is concerned with getting
facts before the American people as to the changes which
are affecting our human resources and our natural resources.
On the subject of this change in population they have many
vital figures and information as to trends with which you
should be concerned. . . .

The purpose of the planning councils among the States and
of the National Resources Committee is to get the facts as
to these conditions before business people in a way that will
open their eyes and make them appreciate the necessity of the
conservation of our natural resources. . . . This is all a part
of the planning program, a reason why business should be
giving its support to that movement. . . .

DEMOCRATIC TREND TOWARD EFFICIENCY [14]

It is no accident that there is not one example in history
where a democratic government transmuted itself into a dictatorship by the process of becoming more and more efficient or
more effective in meeting economic problems. Such a change
in governmental system comes only through a sharp convulsion,
a sharp breaking off of old ways, and a new start in a different
direction.

Hence to my mind the most irresponsible and dangerous
type of demagoguery that is abroad in the land today is the
attempt of some people to make the American people believe

[14] From discussion on the floor of the House of Representatives, by Hon. Jerry
Voorhis of California. Reprinted in Appendix, *Congressional Record.* 84:3192.
July 12, 1939.

that constructive attempts to make our government more effective and better able to reduce inequalities and deal with unemployment, monopoly, and corruption are steps toward dictatorship because forsooth their democracy, to be constitutional, must be synonymous with inefficiency, lack of planning, and governmental ineffectiveness in dealing with economic problems. Such, I am convinced, does not need to be the case. . . .

OPPOSING ECONOMIC PLANNING

TREND TOWARD GREATER CONTROL [1]

The Brookings Institution, asserting that there was a trend toward government regulation of industrial prices and production, said today that "the more widely such policies are followed, the less is the net benefit" to owners and employers, and "the larger is the cost to the community as a whole." The conclusions were reached in a study of the relationship of government to economic life.

Citing regulation of the bituminous coal industry as an attempt to protect the domestic market of an industry "which finds the demand for its products declining," the report said:

"Short-run gains to coal workers and operators appear possible, but it is improbable that there will be any long-run gains. The use of substitutes is likely to increase, while higher wages may further stimulate mechanization of the industry and force diminution of direct employment.

"Consumers may pay permanently higher prices for the product. More significant, however, is the possibility that government price regulation in such a highly competitive industry cannot be made effective without government control of output."

The study also reached the conclusion that preparation for war "inevitably means greatly augmented government control of economic life. . . ."

Growth of governmental power and responsibilities, the report maintained, has taken place "in such piece-meal fashion that its full import has not been grasped," and as a result "there has been a development of government functions which

[1] From *The New York Times*. June 17, 1940. p. 6. News story.

might not have been approved in its entirety had it been presented as a general program."

THE BUSINESS VIEW [2]

Assuming . . . that the war does come to an early and abrupt end, outlook for the year becomes less favorable from a strictly business viewpoint. Of course, long pull prospects will be greatly enhanced, and the sooner peace does come, the less severe the readjustments, especially in view of the success that business and government have had so far in combating war-time inflation.

In fact it might be added that the policy of the government, with its controls extending into finance, credit and virtually all lines of production, has become so pronounced as to have already suggested the danger, should the war continue, of government influence being extended to a point where it will interfere with the normal and necessary readjustments.

PROTECTION INSTEAD OF PLANNING [3]

The truth is that no economic planning authority could possibly have foreseen, planned, plotted and organized such an amazing spectacle of industrial progress as the world has witnessed in the last century. No trust or combination, private or governmental, could have accomplished it. It could have been achieved only under conditions where there was a wide open invitation to all the genius, inventive ability, organizing capacity and managerial skill of a great people. Nobody must

[2] By B. K. Price, associate editor, Steel magazine. From "War and Politics." Steel. 106:152-3. Jan. 1, 1940. Reprinted by permission.
[3] By J. Howard Pew, president, Sun Oil Company. From "Planned Economy; Dangers." Bankers Magazine. 138:290. April 1939. Reprinted by permission.

be barred, no invention rejected, no idea untried; everybody must have his chance; and under our American system of free enterprise and equal opportunity everybody gets just that chance. It is our freedom that has brought us to this high estate. . . . With so many political witch doctors abroad in the land teaching communism, fascism, planned and dictated economies, governmental paternalism and all the others, I urge you to guard well that heritage and turn a deaf ear to all their sophistries. When a people come to look upon their government as the source of all their rights, there will surely come a time when they will look upon that same government as the source of all their wrongs. That is the history of all planned, dictated economies. That is the history of tyranny. . . . It is not unthinkable that in the light which shows through this twentieth century, a great progressive people will be beguiled into turning back to the ways of controlled economies and dictated social programs.

Government can help by safeguarding the common man's right to be himself—all of himself. It can protect against monopoly, tyranny, extortion, and every infringement of human rights. When it shall have done this much, it will have served its highest purpose.

THE THREAT OF EMERGENCY POWERS [4]

The transition from a form of government which confines its prerogatives to the protection of these rights to a form of government which imposes a planned economy on its nationals may be quite as unnoticeable as it is insidious. . . . It has its genesis usually in the necessity of some economic crisis within the state, or in the fear of war from without. In either case, realizing that prompt action is necessary against a common

[4] By Wood Netherland, vice-president, Mercantile-Commerce Bank & Trust Company, St. Louis, Mo. "What Profiteth It a Nation?" *Vital Speeches.* 5:753-5. Oct. 1, 1939. Reprinted by permission.

foe, citizens of a democracy entrust their leaders with certain emergency powers "to provide for the common defense"—and thus in a spirit of patriotism voluntarily forego rights which under normal circumstances they reserve sacredly unto themselves. At the time of this foregoing there is no thought of giving up inherent natural rights indefinitely, but usually, to use the stock phrase, it is "for the duration of the emergency." The grave danger of this departure from these basic tenets of a free people is that either the laws voted in an emergency are seldom repealed, or the period of the emergency is so prolonged that the restrictions which tend to stifle fundamental rights become a permanent and accepted part of our political economy. . . .

I have said that the transition from a democratic form of government to one which dictates a planned economy, usually makes its greatest strides during periods of national emergency. A pertinent case in point is the necessity for national unity now confronting us as a result of the war in Europe. . . .

It seems to me we have gone a long way on this transition from our original conception of a free government to one which dictates a planned economy, and that it is high time we pull over to the side of the road, shut off the engine for a while, and have a look at our compass.

THE CHOICE BEFORE US [5]

It is curious that even in a country like ours, where the overwhelming majority of the people are against state socialism and where the socialists have never been able to poll a very large vote, many groups support more or less actively, or regard with indifference, measures similar to the N.R.A. and the A.A.A. which added one by one, arrive at the goal of state socialism.

[5] By Millard E. Tydings, U.S. Senator from Maryland. From "How Far Should Government Control Business?" *Vital Speeches.* 5:295. Mar. 1, 1939. Reprinted by permission.

In other words, people are opposed to state socialism as a whole but accept with complaisance the rapidly multiplying steps which lead directly to it.

Thus we have in America people who favor government ownership of power companies but who are opposed to government ownership of farms or government domination of business generally. Without forming a clear-cut idea of the functions of government, they stand in the camp favoring government operation and in the camp opposed to it, at one and the same time. . . .

Free enterprise on the one hand and state socialism on the other will not long survive together in the same country. One is sure to perish. We must make our choice. To put it differently: We must choose between voluntary cooperation on the one hand and compulsory operation on the other.

CONTROLLED ECONOMY VERSUS FREE SOCIETY [6]

Pressures operating against free enterprise—free business enterprise— . . . come from two sources: First, those who are erroneously designated as economic planners but who have something in mind quite different from planning, namely, governmental control of the processes of production and distribution; secondly, from minority groups of business men. . . .

Those who favor governmental control of our economy have as their avowed objectives happiness and a more abundant life for the masses. A worthy goal most certainly, but one utterly unattainable by the methods they propose unless all past history is no guide to the future.

I do not question the sincerity of the economic planners who believe, almost to the point of fanaticism, that the more abundant

[6] By Paul G. Hoffman, president, Studebaker Corporation. From "Free Private Enterprise—Can It Survive?" *Vital Speeches*. 5:205-8. Jan. 15, 1939. Reprinted by permission.

life can be realized by rigid governmental controls. But there is one very curious thing about them. They say, and apparently believe, that this doctrine of theirs is new, and that they are the leaders who are courageously carrying the banners of society forward to a wholly new kind of world order.

That is probably one of the very worst things about those who favor governmental control, apart from the viciousness of their doctrine. They have lashed their opponents contemptuously with "horse-and-buggy" epithets, when, as a matter of sheer historical fact, the controls which they are advocating as the latest thing are not new at all, but are as old as government itself. And far more thoroughly out-dated than the horse and buggy. From the days of tribal chiefs right down to the present-day dictators, the idea has persisted among ambitious rulers that they can somehow order the affairs of mankind better than individual men and women can order their own affairs. . . .

Now let us examine for a moment the claim that governmental control of our economy will bring a higher degree of happiness to the masses. I hold the deep conviction that only a people who enjoy civil liberty and religious freedom can be genuinely happy. . . . Speaking historically, civil and religious liberties have always followed the breaking of governmental controls over the market. . . .

Consider why:

Planned economy simply cannot function without rigid price and production controls. A free people will not tolerate such controls over a sustained period of time. They rise in protest and start exercising their individual judgments, thus endangering the success of the plan. The planners have no choice. Civil liberties must be sacrificed or the plan will fail. . . . Coercion is an absolute corollary of planning and control. There is no way to escape it if control is to be successful. The people must obey blindly. Each one is given his quota and he must like it—or if he doesn't like it, obey anyway. A planned and controlled economy cannot operate within the fabric of a free society. . . .

I have some fairly definite ideas as to what business should do to fortify the competitive economy and what it cannot do without weakening it. . . .

Business must establish a sound relationship with government. We must recognize that public interest is always the paramount consideration and that it is the task of government to protect it. In a considerable area of our economy the public is best served by enterprises which are monopolistic. Quite obviously, these natural monopolies must be under governmental regulation. In a far wider area of our economy, the force of competition is of itself the best protection of public interest. When we talk of free enterprise, we are thinking of this large segment. Here, the government has the broad responsibility of laying down ground rules that will protect the public against fraudulent practices; that will protect one competitor against the unfair advantages of another; and that will prevent restraint of trade by private monopoly. . . .

Over a long period, the Federal Trade Commission has been at work steadfastly and quietly at the task of safeguarding free enterprise against the type of competition that would destroy competition iself.

Limited to a narrow authority, it has been a factor far beyond its actual orders in getting business to accept its responsibilities. . . .

The Department of Justice is charged with the primary responsibility of battling against monopolistic practices. The efforts now being made to clarify the laws on monopoly and restraint of trade are commendable. . . .

To sum up my thinking as to the relationship between government and business in the competitive area where free enterprise should prevail, I hold that business should work wholeheartedly with government in maintaining competition in the cooperative system. . . . I hold that it is an important part of management's job to do everything in its power to establish employment and to pay the best possible wages because it is good business to do so. I hold that all decent management should welcome laws placing on all industry the obligation of workmen's compensation, unemployment insurance and old age pensions. I discard as archaic the notion that such measures of mass security should be left to the benevolent whim of the private employer. . . . The security of workers should not be dependent upon private business because private business is too precarious.

Next comes labor. Business has, in my opinion, a very real responsibility toward its workers. . . . We must work together, and we must make collective bargaining work, and thus take industrial relations out of the realm of politics. . . .

Finally, I propose giving my views on what businessmen must *not* do. They must cease and desist from asking for special privilege of any kind from local, state, or national governments. . . . It is an act of treachery and business suicide as well, because special privilege is an invitation to governmental control, and no business can long survive bureaucratic domination. . . . Insist that free enterprise be kept free in America.

THE ILLUSION OF ECONOMIC PLANNING [7]

There is one magnificent obsession that I feel I must nominate for the label of an illusion. . . . It is economic planning. Sometimes it is called planned economy and sometimes national economic planning. What it boils down to, when and if it reaches the stage of concrete measures, is coercive regimentation of all business and government under a few bureaucrats who owe their position and power to one or more politicians. It is one of the things that the Founding Fathers sought to escape

[7] By Mark M. Jones, president, Akron Belting Company and consulting economist. "Hope or Fear." *Vital Speeches.* 5:424. May 1, 1939.

and prevent, yet recently it has been brought forth beautifully streamlined. As we know too well, it has been avidly taken up by persons who for the most part can find no other way to make a living. Moreover, it is now the fashion in certain political and bureaucratic circles to propagate it on every possible occasion. But it still remains the same ancient fallacy that time and again has been discredited at an incalculable cost in human blood, treasure and misery. It cannot be national, it will not be economic, and there would be no real planning in it. Just the heel of a few politicians on the neck of the people.

NO SOLUTION IN PLANNING [8]

Few persons seem to realize how far economic conditions in this country are due, not only to the Great War of 1914, and the international policies and disturbances which followed, but also to monetary management and economic planning by our own governmental authorities. Until twenty-five years ago we had on the whole a free economy, subject to the laws but not to the management of government authorities. But since the United States entered the war in 1917, the government has in large measure managed our money and planned our economy. . . .

It is our duty, not to criticize, but to learn from experience, not to waste time justifying or blaming past decisions, but to weigh them and their effects for our future guidance. . . .

We should have cooperation between business and government. And I mean cooperation, not dictation by government, nor vituperation by business. No economy can work well when business and government are at loggerheads.

[8] By R. C. Leffingwell, partner, J. P. Morgan & Company. From "U. S. Price Program Seen as Beating Back Revival in Business." *Printers' Ink*. 190:14+. Reprinted by permission.

We need cooperation between government, management and labor, to increase the output, and the efficiency, and the real income, of labor as a whole. . . .

We should have taxes for revenue only, and not to penalize thrift, or to distribute or destroy wealth, or to stop trade. We should not increase taxes. . . .

Finally, I believe we have had twenty-two disturbed years and a ten-year depression, we have idle men and idle dollars, partly because our money was managed and our economy has been planned by government.

The American economy isn't worn out. We are in our adolescence as a people. We have only scratched the surface of the resources of this great continent. . . .

I suspect that the more money is managed, the more economy is canalized and regimented, the more the individual is controlled by government—then so much the more the national economy will run down hill, will deteriorate and be depressed, at first slowly to be sure, then faster and faster, until the rulers of that economy are forced to seek more desperate remedies, more autocratic powers.

PLANNED ECONOMY VERSUS FREE GOVERNMENT [9]

When a critic refers to the New Deal scarcity philosophy he is attacking the theory of economic planning, economic control, regimentation, communism, socialism, and fascism. The fundamental significance of each is the same. Each represents an abandonment of the principle of economic progress through operation of free competitive enterprise and free government. . . . The legislative program of the New Deal is taking us down to a completely "planned economy. . . ."

[9] From discussion on the floor of the House of Representatives, June 16, 1938, by Hon. Roy O. Woodruff of Michigan. Reprinted in Appendix, *Congressional Record*. 83:2989-91. June 17, 1938.

A major objection to the economic planning and scarcity theory of the New Deal is that control of one economic activity or one industry soon leads to the control of all economic life, and eventually to the complete domination of all political activity. . . . Control, once established, is never suppressed until it becomes all-inclusive. This is nowhere better illustrated than under the A.A.A. The attempt to control the production of seven basic commodities led to the successive control of thirteen major farm products. Control in the first instance was of acreage only, but now production and marketing are both controlled. . . .

When the planner succeeds in substituting his decisions for those of sound economic processes, he will have achieved control over the economic and political life of the country. His decisions would influence elections. He could make or break an industry. He could force minorities into line. . . .

The effects on government are even more serious. It is often pointed out that the inevitable end of economic planning is a change in the form of government from a constitutional republic to a totalitarian state. In the latter, power no longer rests with the people, but with a dictator. . . .

A planned economy is opposed to the constitutional separation of powers. Under it decisions must be made quickly. Complete power must be given the executive. The processes are so complex. Consequently, Congress must delegate a wide range of power to the executive. . . .

Home rule, or states' rights, must go, so that a planned economy with master minds can rise triumphant in its place. . . . Those who think that a planned economy or economic dictatorship will not eventually lead to a political dictatorship should note the following statement of Professor Cassel, a distinguished Swedish scholar, who has had ample opportunity to observe this inevitable tendency: "Once authoritative control has been established, it will not always be possible to limit it to the economic domain."

The policy of the federal government should be to encourage business to produce as much as it possibly can. If prices are low, based on low cost of production, so much the better; for as prices are decreased the consumer will have found a real increase in the purchasing power of his dollar and therefore an increased real income.

GOVERNMENT CONTROL UNSATISFACTORY [10]

Since the war there has been a world-wide trend toward more government control of business. In our own country material progress, as measured by indexes of production, has been less rapid than before the war. Ups and downs have been more severe. Unemployment has been great. This unsatisfactory condition cannot be attributed entirely to the increase in governmental powers. The disjointed state of affairs produced by the war necessitated some intervention of government. Many governmental measures have been helpful under the circumstances. But it is clear that the results of an increased degree of central management of economic forces have not been entirely satisfactory. The comparison of recent progress with prewar progress is not favorable.

Very few businesses can operate with success upon the basis of central plans projected very far into the future. . . . Where are we to find the central planners who can foresee inventions before the inventors, who can predict changes in styles, demand and weather, can forecast the influence of wars or other extraneous developments, or can be intimately familiar with all the details of all business? . . .

There are a few economic matters which could conceivably be centrally guided with a high degree of success, provided the

[10] By J. W. Howe. From "Economic Planning and Capital Values: Why Government Control Is Unsatisfactory." *Annalist*. 52:69. July 13, 1938. Reprinted by permission.

personnel in charge of them was ideal in character and specialized training and was never compelled to yield to political expediency. I refer principally to bank credit. But even here the precedents are not altogether happy. It is not possible for money management to control any single economic factor such as the price level, or the degree of business activity, in the manner or to the extent that many have hoped. Even perfect management of money could not of itself correct all economic maladjustments. It would merely be rather helpful.

In practice most economic decisions must be based upon opinion and upon trial and error. Such opinions ought to be based upon the intimate first-hand knowledge of the many details of particular enterprises. Success requires the power of flexibility, speed of decision, quick change and adaptation to altered conditions. Economic forces cannot in general be made to conform to cumbrous standardized rulings and laws of government. The laws must bend to economic forces. Hence, by leaving economic forces free to work themselves out under competitive conditions without and radical or over-ambitious attempts at central management, we undoubtedly attain the finest practical adjustment of conditions, the best dispersion of prosperity and the most rapid progress. At least, a comparison of the record of the nineteen years before the war and the record of the nineteen years since so indicates.

It must be admitted that there is no way at present of avoiding some central management of the supply of bank credits and of tariffs. But by limiting the scope of central management to these and to the government's own business we can reduce the uncertainties which arise from the impossibility of predicting what the central manager will do. We then make it possible to do business upon the basis of a study of one's own business and general economic conditions, for central planning, paradoxically, impedes individual planning. If the objectives of such central management as is unavoidable is to prevent violent changes, and as far as possible to permit the free action of econ-

omic forces, we shall have a surer basis for progress than if
it contemplates radical changes upon the basis of concepts based
upon limited statistical averages.

The attempt at central management has been expensive everywhere.   The expenditures of our own federal government are
more than ten times as great as they were before the war.   The
expenditures of all our government bodies are equal to about
25 per cent of last year's national income. . . .

MORE POWER IN THE PEOPLE [11]

No absorption of power by centralized government should
be permitted through subterfuge or indirection.   No power of
the people or of the states should be delivered to the federal
government which is not openly recognized and approved by the
Supreme   Court   or   through   constitutional   amendment.   The
increase of federal authority in government must be matched
by an increase in all types of governmental authority, or the
power now held through centralized government should be restored to the states and through the states to local agenices of
government. . . .   No task should be committed to the government which can better be performed through cooperative action
of the people in a voluntary and private way. . . .

American freedom and essential equality are now being chal-
lenged chiefly in the market place.   Industry and labor are
logical partners, but it was never intended that government and
industry should be partners, for they have different responsibilities, and such a partnership ignores the rightful place of labor
as a partner.   The partnership of government and industry is
a Fascist idea; it is currently being demonstrated in the Fascist
states of Europe.

[11] From address by Hon. James J. Davis, of Pennsylvania, Dec. 17, 1938.
Reprinted in *Congressional Record*. 84:21-2. Jan. 5, 1939.

The American ideal is the partnership of labor and industry in the task of production and distribution, with government to serve as an impartial referee in case of disputes and to insure fair play. . . . No interference with the economic processes of production or distribution by the government, under the American system, should be tolerated except for emergency needs, and these should not be encouraged to last forever. . . .

The remedy for an overexalted power of state is more power in the people. For the government is not the people but of the people, by the people and for the people. . . . We have tried the roads of restricted production and planned scarcity. These have failed. . . . Peace comes with plenty not poverty. Goodness comes with abundance, not starvation.

THE IMPOSSIBILITY OF A DEMOCRATIC PLANNED ECONOMY [12]

Because economic difficulties have beset us in recent years, the path of least resistance has been to let the government try to solve our problems for us. The thought is often expressed that the free enterprise system has failed because we still have unemployment, distress and periodic maladjustments. Therefore, it is argued, the government must "do something"—on the assumption that anything new will be better than the status quo. This is an understandable psychological reaction, but the road, I fear, will lead to a goal we would not knowingly seek. . . .

Government planning . . . means the destruction of individual initiative and self-realization. When one is told what price one can charge, what profit one can make, what work one can do, there is neither the motive nor the opportunity for individual growth and advancement.

[12] By Winthrop W. Aldrich, chairman, Board of Directors, Chase National Bank, New York City. "The Incompatibility of Democracy and a Planned Economy." *Vital Speeches*. 5:531-4. June 15, 1939. Reprinted by permission.

A government undertaking delicate price dictation which vitally affects the life and welfare of all its citizens could tolerate no criticism. When price decisions are made by government planners, someone is bound to be dissatisfied. If the number of aggrieved persons is large and if the state permits them to cry out that injustice has been done, the enforcement of decisions will be next to impossible. . . . Thus government economic planning requires the suspension of individual judgment concerning what is wise or not.

Under a planned economy, because of the impossibility of reconciling all conflicting interests to the satisfaction of all concerned, the welfare of the individual is considered to be unimportant; the individual must be submerged for the good of the "cause." . . .

Government planning inevitably leads to intolerance of minority views and a disregard of minority rights. A government regulating all the details of economic life and doing all the thinking for its people cannot stop at legal technicalities protecting minority interests. . . .

The enforcement of the price decisions requires a large and very efficient corps of secret police—and a secret police visiting at any time homes, stores, factories, warehouses with a carte blanche for exploratory investigations, violates the very essence of democratic principles. Yet without such an enforcement staff, the innumerable detailed and specific price decrees would be honored far more in the breach than in the observance. We have seen in the last few years in our own country the breakdown of an attempt to fix industrial prices and production on a large scale—and the breakdown was due to the fact that . . . producers could not be "kept in line." Enforcement in a democratic way proved impossible.

Still another ramification of a governmentally priced economy is that equality of all citizens cannot exist. The government planners and administrators become a specially privileged class. . . . "Party" members—all believers in the wisdom and justness of the decisions of the planners—are also endowed with special favors and prerogatives.

Furthermore, government "planning" necessitates radical changes in the techniques of government. The whole concept of representative democratic government implies that the power of a state must be limited to its capabilities, and limited to the ability of the people to exert effective control. If government is set apart from the people or above them their interest in its direction is dissipated in a mass of technicalities. When a state grows powerful enough to direct the details of economic life, it becomes a political octopus too complex for popular comprehension, and too omnipotent for popular control. . . .

Furthermore, representative government is not organized for effective economic regimentation. A large elected assembly is too cumbersome and unwieldy for effective action in designing, executing, and enforcing plans. A Congress of 531 men cannot decide how many shoes should be produced, how much cotton will be needed next year, how much electricians should earn a day and so forth. Representatives, no longer able to deliberate and legislate according to the wishes of the electorate "back home," will have to hand over their jobs to "experts" who will give the voters not what the voters want, but what the experts think they should have. When governments attempt to make price decisions, they must be so organized that an individual, or at most a small commission or planning board has the final authority on all matters. Government by law must end when government by administrative "economic planners" begins.

Also, many of the most important economic plans cannot be drawn for one year, but must be made for many years ahead. Once started, they cannot be shifted or abandoned in response to changes in public opinion. Public opinion cannot be permitted to form, and certainly must not be allowed to exert any effective influence on the affairs of state.

Furthermore, a government which even pretends to be responsive to the public will cannot afford to acknowledge its mistakes. Errors, of course, will occur, and the mistakes will be on a grand scale. Under the private planning system, if one person misjudges a market . . . he will suffer and his creditors may have to take some losses, but the economy as a whole, will not be greatly disrupted. If similar errors of judgment are made by a central planning board—and they are much more likely to be made by such a body, because the decisions they have to make are vastly more complex—everyone must pay for the miscalculation, which will be on a gigantic national scale. What actually happens is that government planners never dare admit their errors; they must always cover up to "save face," and in covering up, new mistakes follow the old ones in desperate succession.

If a government attempts to maintain its democratic form, while at the same time it indulges in economic planning . . . the result is government by intrigue, partisanship, and pressure groups. . . .

It is no disparagement of government administrators to say that no man or group of men is capable of being trusted with unrestricted power. Even the best and most socially minded of administrators can become tyrannical if granted dictatorial powers. It is easy to devise plans for a utopian society if one can assume away human fallibility, but such plans are not worth the paper they are written on.

Our economy today is so complex that no one person can have sufficient knowledge to guide and regulate it. No one person can possibly comprehend all the intricate details of our specialized activities. It usually takes a lifetime to master any single sphere of our economic life, be it salesmanship, banking, engineering, office management, or building a house. Furthermore, even the wisest men cannot agree among themselves as to what should be done to improve this or that particular part of our economic organism. They cannot agree on a diagnosis, let alone a cure. We have discovered many facts relative to our economic and social institutions in the last fifty years, but we still do not know enough to make possible successful economic planning by supermen no matter how intelligent, experienced, or socially minded they may be.

For these and many other reasons, I maintain that a democratically "planned economy" is an impossibility. Free enterprise and democracy must fall together, as they arose together.

CAN BUSINESS FIND A SOLUTION?

MANAGEMENT LOOKS AHEAD [1]

I said it seemed to me imperative that business management recognize the dangers of increasing government regulation and control as leading steadily toward central authority and government ownership. This industry has been aware of that danger. Its policy of lower and lower prices for its product, or more and more value for the same money, has certainly been responsible for the good will which the public generally holds toward it. It has not run frantically to government for help against this or that competitive problem; it has encouraged world trade and has asked for little protection for itself.

This is an example which industry generally may well endeavor to follow. Business alone can save the private property system and check the trend toward totalitarianism. . . .

For us as management to hold such views doesn't mean we're turning pink or selling out; it only means that we are determined to have the leadership which belongs to us; to win back whatever public confidence we may have lost; to show to the American people that its greatest good lies down the road of private enterprise and not down the road of more and more control by government.

A PATTERN FOR INDUSTRY [2]

It seems clear that the time has now been reached when the community has a right to demand that the intelligence of

[1] By William L. Batt, president, S. K. F. Industries, Inc. From "Management Looks Ahead." *Vital Speeches.* 6:278. Feb. 15, 1940. Reprinted by permission.

[2] By Alfred P. Sloan, Jr., chairman, General Motors Corporation. "Prices, Wages and Hours." *Vital Speeches.* 5:87-8. Nov. 15, 1938. Reprinted by permission.

the nation's representative leadership be brought to bear in the closest of cooperation, that our whole economic position may be reappraised and readjusted so as to promote to the utmost that sound experience and scientific knowledge may make possible, the essential objectives of *more things for more people,* and *the opportunity to work.* . . . While cooperation is important between all the component parts of the economy, it is particularly so between government and the management of industry, for only thus can the most effective rules be established under which the component parts can function among themselves, as well as maintain an economic balance with other groups comprising the economy as a whole. . . .

The viewpoint, the experience and the responsibilities of those concerned in government and of those concerned in the management of industry and business, are necessarily divergent. Neither can be expected to understand properly the problems, the difficulties, the limitations of the other. Therefore, it is only through a frank exchange of viewpoints that a full coordination of national understanding and purpose is possible and the maximum contribution made to the objectives in which we are all so vitally concerned.

What is needed, therefore, is a spirit of friendly cooperation. Whatever form it may take, is immaterial. *Some* form is the point at issue. . . . The Temporary National Economic Committee . . . offers one form of such cooperation, which should have industry's full and aggressive support. . . . So let us build, as far as time permits, a "Pattern for Industry" around the formula, which pattern may be expanded on as broad a front as desired. . . . The only economically sound way toward our objective, namely, the advancement, socially and economically of the American worker, is *through increasing the efficiency of industrial enterprise.* . . .

In other words, we must encourage a more intensive capitalization of technical progress. We must increase the productivity per worker. Then the higher wage rate can be sustained without increasing prices, and should result in reduced prices. Increased wages then buy more. Lower prices then bring goods and services within the reach of more buyers. Industry is expanded. The standard of living advances. An acceptance of this simple economic truth would be a real forward step.

PLANNED ECONOMY BY INDUSTRY [3]

An "industrially planned" economy by those who are responsible for what we call our private economy. . . . That is the planning which must be done by industry and finance if our industrial order is to survive. It is futile for us to proclaim our industrial system as the best in the world; futile for us to boast of its accomplishment in producing in the past the highest standard of living in the world. That will not preserve the system unless we find the way to prevent the recurrence of more-than-nine-year-long periods of unemployment, distress and despair for millions of people. If the system is to be preserved we must find the way to secure orderly and continuous operation of industry and employment of labor. The way will not be found by politicians pandering for votes. It will not be found by well intentioned but inexperienced theories. If it is to be found at all it must be found by the careful study and diligent search of those who have built our industrial machine and who ought to be able to find the way to make it work, not by fits and starts, but efficiently and continuously.

Of this we may be sure. Unless we find the way, politicians and theorists will continue to try to find it. Our protests and condemnation of their plans will not avail to prevent their efforts.

[3] By William T. Nadin, chairman of the board, Federal Reserve Bank of St. Louis. Speech. From *Commercial and Financial Chronicle*. 148:3465. June 10, 1939. Reprinted by permission.

There has been from time to time a good deal of hopeful expression that industry and government were showing signs of a more cooperative attitude. Cooperation . . . is alive and useful only when applied to a definite purpose and plan. We have the purpose. We all desire to be cured of our ailments. But where is the plan? With what are we to ask the government to cooperate? With nothing but the theory that if the government will abandon its activity designed to cure our ills, the ills will cure themselves? Who among us can believe that we shall get such cooperation? With what are we to cooperate? With a governmentally-planned economy? Who expects that to be done or believes that permanent prosperity could come from it?

On the other hand, who is so pessimistic as to conclude that cooperation could not now be secured by industry, by labor, and by the government if the brains which so well mastered the art of producing material things turned upon the problem of producing them in orderly, continuous fashion, offered a plan of future operations which unquestionably disclosed the purpose, and gave reasonable promise of the result of avoiding in the future such disasters as came upon us nine and a half years ago and still continue with us?

THE CHALLENGE TO INDUSTRY [4]

Industry today is face to face with an unprecedented challenge. It has to create a better livelihood for the American people; and, at the same time, it has to produce the materials for a national defense which will insure national survival.

But these two tasks are really, at bottom, the same task. We cannot create a better livelihood for the American without an effective economic system; and without an effective economic

[4] From *Factory Management and Maintenance*, Section A. 98:1-5. Aug. 1940. Reprinted by permission.

system, we cannot competently and sufficiently produce the materials for our national defense.

Today, as never before in our history, American industry must strive toward an effective American economic system in the name both of prosperity and of patriotism.

We who are familiar with industry know that *if it is given the right conditions* it can create goods and services almost illimitable for the American people and can provide them with a defense equipment that no foreign foe will ever be able to penetrate . . . *if it is given the right conditions.*

Ah, that "if!" . . . Those conditions do not exist. Why? Because most Americans are following economic delusions. . . . The great immediate job of American industry is therefore a missionary job . . . to persuade the American people to turn from delusions to verities. . . . American industry *must* do this missionary job—*or perish.*

The European totalitarian countries shriek this truth at us. The people of those countries were devastated with war, waste, inefficiency, unemployment. They did not thereupon turn to industry. They turned to government. They called in the government to bind industry in chains. Influenced by a combination of genuine suffering and of false argumentation, they introduced a governmental planned economy and they exterminated free enterprise.

That same process has now begun among us. We have genuine suffering among our industrial unemployed and among our agricultural migrants. We have false argumentation directed by powerful voices against all industry and all industrialists. We have government measures designed not to increase wealth but to share poverty. We have cunning governmental schemes for first crippling industry and for then blaming industry for not marching. We have propaganda day and night for making industry unpopular and for training the people to believe that government is their only savior. . . .

We cannot have economic *civil war* between American groups and also have American prosperity and American national military safety. We have to get together in a free national unity that will be stronger than any of the world's *enslaved* national unities.

WHAT AMERICANS THINK

What do the men who are leaders in American life think of the necessity for economic planning? To answer that question, the compilers of this book wrote to a number of men prominent in business, education, and political affairs, and asked each of them the following two questions:

First, do you believe that the present international situation demands a greater degree of control by the national government over industry than has previously existed?

Second, aside from the present emergency, do you think that such increased control is desirable in the interests of long-range planning or for other reasons?

The answers received are quoted verbatim, in the following pages—*The Compilers*.

A democracy is dependent upon cooperative effort from all sources, and any formula that brings the greatest good for the prosperity of our country, I would subscribe to most heartily. Careful study and good old common sense in designing a formula should by its very nature meet wartime conditions and serve well toward long range planning.——*Thomas L. Smith, president, Standard Brands Incorporated.*

The need of uniform labor standards, across state lines, in an industrial system that is increasingly nationalized, makes increased national control of industry desirable and necessary even in normal times.

In time of national emergency calling for increased and sustained production of special materials, it is imperative that the national government increase its control over industry. This is strikingly illustrated in the recruiting of labor when shortages occur in the labor supply in various industries. The government must prevent employers from stealing skilled workmen away from each other, as happened during early months of the first Great War. The government alone can enforce the economical and expeditious distribution of skilled workers to the more essential industries. For this purpose, in extreme necessity, it prohibits employers from advertising for workers and from recruiting through fee-charging employment agencies. Recruiting must be centralized through one labor market—the public employment office system.——*John B. Andrews, secretary, American Association for Labor Legislation.*

If war comes, there will be the necessity for greater control in certain directions than now exists, though even in that case there ought to be a great deal less control than now exists with respect to other points. What we want in a case of that sort is full functioning concentrated on war objectives; but many of the restraints that the federal government imposes today prevent full functioning and ought to be relaxed.

I think that the federal government should make a great retreat from its efforts of managing economic life, aside from the present emergency.——*Benjamin M Anderson, Jr., professor of economics, University of California.*

On the question of the greater degree of control by government over industry than has previously existed, the international situation at present does not admit of any definite statements as to what controls or regulations may be necessary when peace returns. The one thing that seems certain is that there will be a wider extension of government control over industry and foreign trade in other countries and that in our trade, over large areas of the world, we will be confronted with government monopolies.——*Eugene P. Thomas, president, National Foreign Trade Council, Inc.*

It is apparent that regardless of wartime emergencies, the government now has more control over some of the details of business than seems advisable. All realize that the present war conditions demand that labor, business, finance and agriculture must to a certain degree, put national defense and welfare of the republic before their own interests or the professions of which they are a part. National defense comes first. Profiteering on the part of business, or sit-down strikes on the part of labor are steps against the national welfare. Agriculture must likewise put the national interest foremost.

Free enterprise is the foundation of national prosperity. Some regulation is made necessary because of the size of great corporations, but we insist on a minimum of regulation from Washington or elsewhere in agriculture, business and labor. We must demand the largest possible measure of self control. The time has come when labor, business and agriculture must sit around the council table and recognize the interest of all, and the dependence of one upon the other. The government should always be the arbiter in disputes. It should be the referee and the umpire, but never the dictator.——*L. J. Taber, master, National Grange.*

I am unaware of any reason at the present time which would make such control by the government seem necessary. Should it actually become necessary at any time because of an emergency threatening the safety of the American people, I would expect the government to take such action as might be deemed necessary in the circumstances.

I do not consider such control desirable. Further, I consider such control by the government to be definitely at variance with the economic system which we in this country adopted or accepted in the beginning and have followed more or less closely ever since,—a system under which the people as a whole in my opinion have enjoyed a higher standard of living and at the same time greater individual freedom than has been the case in any other country in the world at any time.——*Daniel Willard, president, Baltimore and Ohio Railroad Company.*

The present international situation is fraught with danger
not only to those countries which are now involved in a struggle
to gain military supremacy over their adversaries, but to nations
like the United States which conceivably might be sucked into
the orbit of war. War has made the problem of national defense paramount in this country. National defense has raised
to the fore innumerable matters relating to the functioning of
our national economy, such as production, distribution, and the
elimination of unemployment.

Obviously, there is already a greater degree of control by
government over industry than was previously the case. Whether
such control is desirable—now and later—depends upon how it
is exercised.

If government control of industry is applied in a manner
calculated to bring the greatest good to the greatest number,
then I see no reason for objecting to it. If, on the other hand, a
few greedy profiteers utilize government for their own ends, to
the detriment of the majority of the populace, then increased
government control of industry spells danger to American democracy.

Government has a monopoly on distributing our mail. We
have no objection to that. Many municipalities monopolize the
distribution of water and other utilities. There is no objection
to that. If and when we decide that our federal government
must begin to bring more order into our economic life, then
there certainly should be no objection on that score. So long
as we have the ballot, so long as we exercise our suffrage rights,
so long as we maintain our civil liberties, so long will we, the
people, be able to control our government.—*A. F. Whitney,
president, Brotherhood of Railroad Trainmen.*

"I believe that the present international situation demands
a greater degree of control by the national government over
industry than has previously existed. Republics since the days
of Cicero traditionally have concentrated authority in the chief
magistrate in any time of crisis. Lincoln exercised extra-consti-

tutional power during the Civil War. Great emergency powers were delegated to Wilson in the last World War. Under the so-called New Deal, peacetime emergency powers have been granted to President Roosevelt. I think he has exercised them to the full. But they have been exercised not primarily for national safety, but rather to transfer our economic system for a type of new social order which has been the dream of certain of his half socialistic inner circle. This has resulted in weakening and antagonizing industry rather than regimenting it for a specific national emergency. There are expressions of fear that war powers once granted to the President will permanently destroy what is left of our national economy. I think it is much less dangerous to grant such powers in wartime than in peacetime, for when such powers are granted for the duration of a war, the practice has been to return them to the people after the war is over.

The only real answer to the present situation is for Congress to declare war against Germany and her allies and do it as soon as possible.—*Everett Dean Martin, professor of social philosophy, Graduate School, Claremont College.*

It seems inevitable that a greater degree of control by government will result from the present international situation. Threatened with shortages of such vital materials as rubber and tin, high industrial managers have urged the government to stock these materials in large amounts and also to promote by investment and research the production of substitutes. Their feeling, as far as I can learn, is that the risks of loss are too great for any private interest to bear.

Continuation of such control beyond an emergency created by war or thought of war, does not, however, seem to me advisable. That method of maintaining scientific and industrial progress may work quite well in a nation accustomed to regimentation; but the masses are too energetic and individualist for it to succeed here. My feeling is we originate improvements faster on the basis of individual and group responsibility and reward. An example can be drawn from the automobile industry. In motorizing warfare Germany has merely developed another side of an industry which we pioneered from beginning to end as free men within about forty years.—*Arthur Pound, state historian and economist, State Education Department, University of the State of New York.*

In my opinion, the principal requirements of our defense program are a two-ocean navy and an adequate air defense. There are other considerations, but they are supplementary. A two-ocean navy assumes the possible collapse of the British navy. No greater degree of control, by government, over industry is necessary to meet these requirements. Any radical increase in such control would be harmful.

Long-range planning requires some supermen for planners. I would not know where to get them. For example, I have spent my life in this business and I think I know something about it, but if any man or group of men were to attempt long-range planning for the entire farm implement industry the results would not be comparable with those which obtain under the existing system of free competition.

There is no magic in government control. Government is made up of human beings, generally selected by political processes. In the very nature of things, they cannot possess the qualifications of those who have "learned the business" and whose positions have been attained through demonstrated merit. And also, the system imposed by government, and probably necessarily imposed, precludes any such efficiency as that attained in private industry.—*Burton F. Peek, vice president, Deere & Company.*

The existing international situation requires, not a generalized increase of government control over all industry, but nevertheless any legally warranted measure of control over industries related to defense and to potential wartime operations that may be deemed essential to promoting the country's security and military efficiency. It is not easy to generalize about increased government control in ordinary times of peace. More control may prove desirable in relation to particular (especially newer) industries. But I do not subscribe to the notion that a maximum of government control over industry is the thing to be sought. My own opinion is that under the New Deal government has gone rather too far in this direction, and that our national recovery has been retarded by the heavy hand of government regulation, and perhaps even more by industry's uncertainty as to the further degrees and forms of regulation that may be in store for it. Fully recognizing the necessity for reasonable degrees of public regulation in such fields as utilities and sale of securities, I nevertheless hope to see large liberty maintained for private initiative, management, and enterprise.—*Dr. Frederic A. Ogg, political scientist, University of Wisconsin.*

Whatever difficulties our defense program has encountered so far have not been due to any lack of national control. Even in the case of certain international patent rights the problem, I believe, is not so much of the degree of control as of the absence of any control. Since the reports from everywhere are that industry is cooperating with the government to the utmost, it is obviously preferable to get along with as little increased control and bureaucracy as possible.

Under a socialist economy there undoubtedly will be need of further extension of governmental control for the purpose of long-range planning. But do we want a socialist economy? Under our existing economy the question can be determined only in terms of specific industries and undertakings.—*Abraham Epstein, executive secretary, American Association for Social Security, Inc.*

In time of war or threatened war it is probable that the government would seek absolute power to regulate every business in the United States and do exactly what a government would do under a socialist plan of life. I do not believe that such arbitrary powers are necessary.

There should be a complete plan for mobilization of those resources which have a direct relation to war, but I believe practically every object could be accomplished by permitting the continued operation of private enterprise. Excessive profits could be controlled by greatly increased taxation. With the powers which exist, and the general patriotic spirit of cooperation existing in wartime, I believe the government could obtain all the production, transportation, and other services which it could obtain under strict compulsion. Even in an army we see the development of a deadening bureaucracy. If the same thing is extended to industrial production, we are likely to find it a serious handicap to the successful prosecution of a war.

In time of peace most federal control over industry is claimed to be justified in the name of progress, but surely we can remedy abuses in our present system without taking over the regulation of everything and everybody. Surely the federal government can help work out problems by cooperative efforts with the industries concerned, the states and local governments, without orders from a federal bureau. It may take longer; it may not be so easy; but in the long run it will mean a much more permanent solution, backed by an educated public opinion. The solution is much more likely to stick if it has that kind of support, founded in the sincere cooperation of all concerned, than if it rests on some tyrannical order from a distant capital.— *Robert A. Taft, Senator from Ohio.*

Radio broadcasting stations are accountable once a year in the renewal of their license, before the Federal Communications Commission, for their stewardship in serving "the public interest, convenience and necessity." If at any time during the

year the Commission has reason to believe that a station has
jeopardized the public interest, it may call the station immediately before it by "setting" its license for hearing. With all
the social controls surrounding radio broadcasting in the po
litical, educational and religious segments of American life,
there is no basis which would justify government stepping in
to control program content and naming what shall be spoken
over the air, and who shall speak and who shall not speak.

The radio industry can best serve the American people in
the present emergency, and in any war emergency, by continu-
ing its private and competitive operation which forces stations to
give to radio listeners those program services they want and
not those someone tells them they must have.

Certainly the broadcasters' patriotic instincts are equal to
those of any other body of honest American citizens. Should
an actual war emergency be upon us, I feel confident that through
collaboration with military and government authorities, stations
can voluntarily subscribe to a set of principles which would
permit the widest freedom and variety of radio service and
yet which, at the same time, would not give information which
would be helpful to an enemy within or without, nor which
would not permit those propaganda tactics which seek to divide
and confuse.

It should be remembered that freedom of radio is one of
those freedoms necessary for the very existence of a democracy.
A democracy, after all, has been defined as the expressed will
of the people, and radio communication today has become perhaps man's most potent force for the expression of ideas and
information and the building of morale, civilian and military.
If through any set of circumstances in a democracy the control
of radio passes over to the government as it has elsewhere, the
diversity of opinion which so vitalizes and yet protects the interests of a democratic people, individually and collectively,
would be extinguished—and we know the black gloom which
this has already brought about in the totalitarian countries. We

must never forget that a state radio means education by the state, religion by the state, information by the state, culture by the state. And what is the "state" in a totalitarian nation? That body of men who have seized power and utilize all channels for the communication of thoughts and ideals to grip the minds and hearts of men for their own self-perpetuation in power.—*Neville Miller, president, National Association of Broadcasters.*

The American Federation of Labor is opposed to any kind of despotic power, but we are not afraid to delegate power to a governmental agency provided responsibility for the exercise of that power is definitely located and the official responsible is subject to democratic controls. If the type of authority delegated is administrative, Labor believes that democratic purposes are further safeguarded by the use of advisory committees on which the groups concerned are represented by persons whom they select and who have *real* opportunity to advise. Whether problems to be dealt with by the method of legislation should be approached from the state or federal level must be determined by the circumstances. Administrative power must be as broad as the problem to be dealt with. The national organization of business operating on an interstate basis and using interstate commerce as a medium to business ends, is the explanation of the reference of an increasing number of labor problems to Congress for action. Not because we believe the Federal Government should have increased power, but because we want the scope of remedy to coincide with the problem, we have asked for federal regulation of certain labor situations.

We believe that democracy itself is tied up with local control of educational opportunities and have resisted any attempt to set up federal control in this field. Even when federal aid is given, the Federation insists that the provision should not carry with it federal control.

In the field of vocational education, we believe that the labor standards involved must be nationally determined and locally enforced, but that control over supplementary and related instruction must be local.

As our nation has grown in size and has developed our economic resources, we have increasingly become active in world markets and hence have expected new information and services from our national government, and have placed new duties and responsibilities upon it. For example, circumstances are such that only our Federal Government can deal effectively with the problem of social security for our citizens. The real problem is not that of balancing local against national government, but to develop the government functions and services that we need and to locate them where they will have adequate authority to accomplish the results desired.

Governmental control to be effective, must be adapted to secure the purposes which the people want, and not follow any theoretical and pre-determined forms. Technology has completely changed our social and economic life, and our government in order to fulfill democratic practices must adapt itself to function in our social and economic structures. Government is something not apart from the rest of life. In it the important thing is to follow democratic principles and procedures regardless of the geographic area covered.—*Statement by President Green, American Federation of Labor's position on "Should the Power of the Federal Government be Increased?" December 13, 1940.*

SELECTED BIBLIOGRAPHY

A list of books chosen to supplement the contents of this volume which includes only excerpts from magazine articles, speeches, pamphlets, etc.

Adams, Arthur B. National Economic Security. 328p. Univ. of Oklahoma Press. Norman, Okla. 1936.

Agar, Herbert. Who Owns America: A New Declaration of Independence. 342p. Houghton Mifflin Co. Boston. 1936.

Amery, Leopold S. The Forward View. 464p. Geoffrey Bles, London. 1935.

Arnold, Thurman W. The Bottlenecks of Business. 319p. Reynal & Hitchcock. New York. 1940.
    The anti-trust laws as a frontline of defense against the seizure of industrial power without the approval of Congress. An unobstructed flow of commerce regulated by strictly enforced anti-trust legislation.

Batchelor, Bronson, ed. The New Outlook in Business. 323p. Harper. New York. 1940.
    A symposium in which 21 big businessmen examine the present situation between business and government.

Baxter, W. J. America Faces a Complete Breakdown of Government and Business. 67p. International Research Bureau. New York. 1939.
    State socialism lies ahead for America. The nation is really bankrupt after the last war and is merely attempting to stave off receivership.

Beard, William. Create the Wealth. 314p. W. W. Norton. New York. 1936.

Bohn, Frank and Ely, R. T. The Great Change: Work and Wealth in the New Age. 373p. Thomas Nelson & Sons. New York. 1935.

Brainard, Dudley S. and Zeleny, Leslie D. Economic and Social Planning. (Their Problems of Our Times, v. 2) 350p. McGraw-Hill. New York. 1936.

The Brookings Institution. The Recovery Problem in the United States. 710p. The Brookings Institution. Washington. 1937.

Burns, Arthur R. The Decline of Competition. 590p. McGraw-Hill. New York. 1936.

Carpenter, Charles E. A Real New Deal. 137p. Univ. of Southern California. Los Angeles. 1936.

Chase, Stuart. Government in Business. 296p. Macmillan. New York. 1935.

———— Rich Land, Poor Land. 361p. Macmillan. New York. 1936.

Childs, Marquis W. Sweden, the Middle Way. 171p. Yale Univ. Press. New Haven, Conn. 1936.

Clark, John M. Social Control of Business. Whittlesey House, McGraw-Hill. New York. 1939.

Examines government control of business through pressure groups; analyzes control and its influences, as well as desirability, with the conclusion that stronger social control is necessary.

Cole, George D. H. Economic Planning. 403p. Knopf. New York. 1935.

Coyle, David. Waste: the Fight to Save America. 96p. Bobbs-Merrill. New York. 1936.

Davis, S. C. America Faces the Forties. 283p. Dorrance. Philadelphia. 1940.

Economic conditions in the United States during the '30's with conclusions as to what may be expected in the '40's and particularly with reference to the direction of our American economy.

Dennison, H. S. and others. Toward Full Employment. 297p. Whittlesey House, McGraw-Hill. New York. 1939.

Methods of dealing with unemployment and long range government planning as a solution, recommending a flexible government policy of public works projects created in accordance with employment needs.

Dickinson, John. Hold Fast the Middle Way: an Outline of Economic Challenges and Alternatives. 239p. Little, Brown. Boston. 1935.

Douglas, Lewis W. The Liberal Tradition: a Free People and a Free Economy. 136p. Van Nostrand. New York. 1935.

Douglas, Paul H. Controlling Depressions. 286p. Norton. New York. 1935.

Dulles, E. L. Depression and Reconstruction. 340p. Univ. of Pennsylvania Press. Philadelphia. 1936.

Editors of the Economist. The New Deal: an Analysis and Appraisal. 149p. Knopf. New York. 1937.

Everett, Samuel. Democracy Faces the Future. 269p. Columbia Univ. Press. New York. 1935.

Ezekiel, Mordecai and Brill, Joseph. $2500 a Year: From Scarcity to Abundance. 328p. Harcourt, Brace. New York. 1936.

Fairchild, Henry P. This Way Out. 89p. Harper. New York. 1936.

Finer, Herman. Mussolini's Italy. 564p. Gollancz. London. 1935.

Fisher, Allan George. Clash of Progress and Security. 234p. Macmillan. New York. 1936.

Gaskill, Nelson B. The Regulation of Competition. 179p. Harper. New York. 1936.

Hall, Robert L. Economic System in a Socialist State. 279p. Macmillan. New York. 1937.

Holcombe, Arthur N. Government in a Planned Democracy. 173p. Norton. New York. 1935.

International Industrial Relations Institute. Regional Study Conference, New York, 1934. On Economic Planning. Ed. by Mary L. Fleddérus and Mary Van Kleeck. 275p. Covici, Friede. New York. 1935.

Kinley, David. Government Control of Economic Life and Other Addresses. 418p. Gregg. New York. 1936.

Laidler, Harry W. A Program for Modern America. 517p. Crowell. New York. 1936.

Lawrence, David. Stumbling Into Socialism and the Future of Our Political Parties. 196p. Appleton-Century. New York. 1935.

Lerner, Max. It Is Later Than You Think. Viking Press. New York. 1938.
    An essay on the philosophy of democratic collectivism, describing the end of classical liberalism and the growing need for planning in the immediate future and analyzing current conditions and trends in our economic system.

Lippincott, Benjamin E., ed. Government Control of the Economic Order: A Symposium. 119p. Univ. of Minnesota Press. Minneapolis. 1935.

Lippmann, Walter. The New Imperative. 52p. Macmillan. New York. 1935.

Loeb, Harold, Production for Use. 106p. Basic Books. New York. 1936.

Loeb, Harold and others. The Chart of Plenty. 180p. Viking Press. New York. 1935.

Lyon, Leverett and others. The National Recovery Administration: an Analysis and Appraisal. (Institute of Economics, Publication no. 60) 947p. The Brookings Institution. Washington. 1935.

McGregor, Alexander G. The Correct Economy for the Machine Age. 256p. Pitman. New York. 1935.

Mills, Ogden L. Liberalism Fights On. 160p. Macmillan. New York. 1936.

——— What of Tomorrow? 151p. Macmillan. New York. 1935.

Moulton, Harold G. Income and Economic Progress. (Institute of Economics, Publication no. 68) 191p. The Brookings Institution. Washington. 1935.

Muller, Helen M., ed. Democratic Collectivism. 161p. Wilson. New York. 1935.

National Resources Planning Board. Our National Resources: Facts and Problems. 44p. Government Printing Office. Washington. 1940.

Parker, Glen Lawson. The Coal Industry: A Study in Social Control. 198p. American Council on Public Affairs. Washington. 1940.

Peek, G. N. and Crowther, Samuel. Why Quit Our Own? 353p. Van Nostrand. New York. 1936.

Rohlfing, Charles C. and others. Business and Government. 605p. Foundation Press. New York. 1935.

Ryder, Ambrose. Partnership Way Out. 189p. Harper. New York. 1935.

Soule, George. The Future of Liberty. 182p. Macmillan. New York. 1936.

Stolberg, Benjamin. Economic Consequences of the New Deal. 85p. Harcourt, Brace. New York. 1935.

Stolper, Gustav. German Economy, 1870-1940. 295p. Reynal & Hitchcock. New York. 1940.

Thomas, Norman. After the New Deal, What? 244p. Macmillan. New York. 1936.

Tugwell, Rexford G. The Battle for Democracy. 330p. Columbia Univ. Press. New York. 1935.

Ware, Caroline F. and Means, Gardiner C. Modern Economy in Action. 244p. Harcourt, Brace. New York. 1936.

Willcox, Oswin W. Can Industry Govern Itself? an Account of Ten Directed Economies. 285p. Norton. New York. 1936.

Wooton, Mrs. Barbara. Plan or No Plan. 360p. Farrar & Rinehart. New York. 1935.

World Social Economics Congress, Amsterdam, 1931. Social Economic Planning in the U.S.S.R. 168p. International Industrial Relations Association. New York. 1931.

Report of the Soviet delegation, giving Soviet views on economic planning in practice in the Soviet Union, including the status of groups within the economy and practical operation of the system.

Zook, M. Alva. Blue Prints of the New Social Order: the Planned Commonwealth. 64p. Alva Zook. Glen Ellyn, Ill. 1935.